THE SIXTH SEAL

CLIFFORD W. KELLY, PH.D.

Stonebridge
Publications

Veneta, Oregon

Published by Stonebridge Publications, 87906 Oak Island Dr. Veneta, OR 97487. website: http://StonebridgePublications.com

Cover Photo: Storms with the lightning illustrations, ID 2972997 © Satori13, Dreamstime.com
For the seal: Blank paper with red wax seal, ID 16154542 © Leigh Prather, Dreamstime.com
Cover Design: Rob Trahan

ISBN 13: 978-1-940473-60-4 paperback
ISBN 13: 978-1-940473-61-1 Ebook

FOREWORD

Hard to say where to begin. Perhaps in the third grade at San Bernardino Christian School, as I narrated the Christmas Play when the microphone failed, but I stayed with it somehow and boomed out the lines all the way to the back row. Or, possibly a couple of years later at a Christian youth camp in Barton Flats where, without knowing it, I had played more sports than anyone else in my age group, and won a gold Elgin watch that I still keep locked away. Or, maybe all the way back to my day of birth when my then single mom, abandoned by my often drunken birth dad, wanted to dedicate me to God, but knew no Scriptures as an unbeliever then, so she did an astrological turn with my birthdate, September 23, 1944, which started with Luke 9:23. Later adding verses 24-25, it ran thus:

> Then He said to them all, "If anyone desires to come after Me, let him deny himself, and take up his cross daily, and follow Me. For whoever desires to save his life will lose it, but whoever loses his life for My sake will save it. For what profit is it to a man if he gains the whole world, and is himself destroyed or lost?"
> — Jesus of Nazareth, c. AD 30 (NKJV)

So there you have it: I was "marked" by Him long before I ever met Him on what was a desperate day for me, October 30, 1979, at the age of 35, just this side of a planned suicide on Halloween the very next day. Without the details, I found my way into a small Assemblies of God church, Lincoln Neighborhood in Stockton, California, around 10 am. I met and confessed my alcoholism and debauchery to a pastor who both looked very much like Gene Wilder and shared the actor's first name, Eugene Kraft, who led me in a simple prayer of commitment to the Lord.

And the rest, as they say, is my personal history – and the inspiration for this book.

Now leap forward to July of 1985, where I am a relatively

newly minted Christian professor of communication at what was then called CBN University, now much more elegantly named, Regent University. My wife and I were having dinner with then 700 Club co-host, Danuta Soderman, and her husband at the time, Kai. Seems as the evening ended, Kai Soderman asked me to come back to his office in their lovely cottage in Chesapeake, Virginia, as he said in a pronounced Swedish accent: "Cliff, I have a Word for you from the Lord." Now I didn't know Kai well and was kind of new at this Christianity stuff, but of course I said okay, and this is what he told me just over 30 years ago:

"The Lord tells me you will write only one book. I don't know its title or what it will be about, but the cover will have storm clouds and lightning on it."

After which, Kai and Danuta bade us good night, and we left with me frankly having forgotten this prophetic declaration. Until May 17, 2015, almost to the exact month, 30 years later.

As I was sitting in my small study where my wife and I live, here in Colorado Springs, Colorado, contemplating the increasingly difficult times I saw the nation and world confronting, I sensed God's Voice say, rather emphatically: "Finish the book now!"

Truth be told, I had dabbled with it beginning in 2008, but could never quite get fired up enough to write it, even though I had taught and thought about End Times, or Eschatology, since I first was saved. Used to even have a "prophecy wall" in my office at University of Pacific back in the 1980s, on which I'd post breaking news pieces each morning, long before digital blogs even existed.

After I heard that Command, notably, the first draft was completed precisely 90 days later, on August 17, 2015. Since then, it has gone through several readings by colleagues, both personal and professional, as it now appears, numerous revisions later.

Dedication

So as I close this introduction of sorts, I have several important people to thank most profoundly for this work. First and foremost is my amazing wife, Suzette, who has for the past 36 years not only been my faithful partner in a not-always-easy life, but most importantly, has held my frequently tired feet to biblical fire by helping me stay true, best I can, to His Words. No man, or teacher especially, could ever ask for more.

Second are my grown kids, Christina and Christopher, whose challenges to my way of seeing things were most always brilliantly crafted and many times very loud, but devoted at core to finding what God wants to say to their uniquely searching and passionate peers among the Millennial generation, about which much has been written. Suffice for now to say I have learned much from them, both writers (in fact, my daughter played an integral role in editing this very book) in various stages of pursuing their dreams of service to their peers, one an honors psychology graduate from Loyola University Chicago and the University of Colorado-Denver, the other finishing his undergraduate degree at Sarah Lawrence College in New York. Both of them all the while waging a heroic battle against Crohn's Disease and other invisible illnesses.

Third are the men and women who have helped me tremendously in the formation of my theological and political worldview. Many books and their gifted authors have been formative of course, including the works of Francis Schaeffer, Josh McDowell, C. S. Lewis (and his mentor, J. R. R. Tolkien), Charles Colson, Erich Sauer, Ravi Zacharias, Dinesh D'Souza, Marvin Olasky, Herbert Titus, Walter Davis, Frank Peretti, Carl F. H. Henry, Joel Rosenberg, Cormac McCarthy, Nancy Pearcey, David Noebel, James Dobson, Del Tackett, and a host of other equally gifted authors whom I have read and whose wisdom has been congealed into my present understanding of things past, present, and future. You will see most of them featured in this work across its ten chapters.

And here a special shout out to the hundreds, or even thousands, of students who have graced my long life and career as a university professor. They have served as a safe haven during times of difficulty, my constant exhortation to keep pursuing the truth, and my personal joy as we shared thousands of times of sheer laughter, sometimes in the middle of lectures, when my addled brain decided to take a time out in the middle of an important point. Love you all so very much – You know who you are. And lest I forget, terribly special mention of my BFF (Best Furry Friend) who invariably brings me great joy and unreserved friendship to all my days: Scout the Wonder Dog.

Next are some very special people who have figured prominently in this particular work, starting with Teresa Ortiz, publishing director at Stonebridge Publications, who, after reading some of my Facebook posts invited me to submit my manuscript for review. God bless her for believing in the message enough to back it with all her resources. Then there is my dear friend, author, and theologian, Robert Velarde. Additionally the brilliant former graduate student and now political scientist, Dr. Pamela Jason, my cracker jack editor, Diane Bales, and copious reviews by David Aikman, Bodie Thoene, and John Wheeler. Further still, another former student and Syrian author who has requested anonymity, plus precious friends who reviewed early drafts of the book and provided both feedback and enormous encouragement. They include Paul and Rita Morrow, Billie Kelly, and Betty Holden, and fellow writers, Marijo Phelps and Sydney Tooman Betts, who are also in the Stonebridge stable of authors. And last, but far from least, are Steve and Wendy Riach, godparents to our children and frankly, a second family. I cannot begin to measure their priceless friendship and frequent prayers and advice.

Finally, a very special vote of thanks goes to Brett Bixler, founder of Mission Coffee Roasters here in Colorado Springs. I cannot say strongly enough how that man and his amazing staff have blessed this old professor, as I would show up most every afternoon to ply my online wares from about 2 p.m. to closing at

6 p.m. That place is so very special to so many, a coffee house that not only sponsors Christian missions around the world, but increasingly serves as a gathering center for folks to meet for conversation, business, conferences, or just about anything else you might think of. And yes, I still drink two shot Americanos, although Brett concocted a special dairy-free iced delight he named appropriately, The Cliff Hanger, which I switched to in the hot summer months.

In closing, I have truly saved the very best for last. When I met my Jewish Messiah on that October morning so long ago, I had no idea my then horrific life could take so many wonderful, rich, at times painful, but inevitably, lovely turns in the years that followed. Words are not sufficient to thank Him, who took me, quite literally, from the edge of death to a radically new life in service to others. The word "Wow" comes to mind, defined by Merriam-Webster as an interjection "used to express strong feeling (as pleasure or surprise)" (Wow, n.d.). This one word, perhaps the best term of all, to describe my eternal and undying gratitude for His rescue of me and His sharing with me so many wondrous things from His Word.

So yeah, that's pretty much it. Except for my life Scripture that so many of my students have heard me repeat so very many times over the years, John 8:31-32 (NKJV):

> Then Jesus said to those Jews who believed Him, "If you abide in My word, you are My disciples indeed. And you shall know the truth, and the truth shall make you free."

The Word of the Lord to us all. Thanks be to God.

Table of Contents

THE SIXTH SEAL

A PRE-WRATH COMMENTARY ON THE END OF HISTORY AS WE KNOW IT

CLIFFORD W. KELLY, PH.D.

Chapter 1: Introduction

The world is on fire, and the Messiah is coming soon.
Or, as the Messiah Himself put it so very clearly: "And behold, I am coming quickly, and My reward is with me, to give to every one according to his work" (Rev. 22:12 NKJV). While that thesis may at first appear like a pretentious, careless, almost clichéd boast to many informed readers of politics and eschatology – or what myself and Dr. Pamela Jason have posited as *political eschatology* (the fusion of theology with cultural and geopolitical analysis) – it is, in point of fact, demonstrably true, as this work will attempt to show.

In it, however, there is a catch. And that catch is found directly in the center of the word, *soon.* Taken from the Greek word, *tachu*, it means "after a short time," or "promptly." Another rendering is "early" or "suddenly," indicating a troubling element of *surprise* (Strong, 2009). My favorite is from Noah Webster's classic American Dictionary of the English Language (1828): "In a short time; shortly after any time specified or supposed, without the usual delay." Jesus powerfully reinforced these various notions when He stated repeatedly, "Therefore be on the alert, for you do not know which day your Lord is coming ... for the Son of Man is coming at an hour when you do not think He will" (Mt. 24:42, 44).

In similar regard, Jesus often likened His Second Coming to that of a "thief" (e.g., Rev. 3:3; 16:15) who will suddenly appear to a world thinking of and looking for anything or anyone but Jesus. He even likened such times to those of Noah, when people were blithely "eating and drinking, marrying and giving in marriage," right up until the day Noah entered the ark, and catastrophe lurked just around the bend in that ancient road (Mt. 24:38 NKJV). And that is precisely the kind of world we live in today – a world caught up in the day-to-day tasks, travels, endless trivia, and mounting travails of an increasingly stress-filled existence that demands all of our time and effort just to get through each day. Little thought of the Messiah's Return. Too much to do. Too much to think about. Too many bills to pay. For some, too many parties to attend. For most, too much of everything – except Him, that is.

But the Bible said there would come a time just like this. With only a little literary license here, it was the prophet Daniel who foretold of a period of history when the world would see a vast and rapid increase of travel and activity, within a virtual explosion of information (cf. Dan. 12:4). And so it seems with the advents of the Internet, the digital revolution, and social media, along with the speed-of-light transfer of information and resources, we are inundated with more things and more thoughts than we can possibly manage in today's helter-skelter world. One survey in "The Huffington Post", for example, showed that Americans are literally obsessed with being busy (Henley, 2011).

So if I were to further describe the times in which we presently live, several ideas come to mind. But one that has always stood out for me is found in the ancient, now well-known proverb, "May you live in interesting times." Arguably originating as an old Chinese curse, it most likely means may you live in exceedingly *difficult times*. We need not look far beyond the devastating contours and consequences of the events of September 11, 2001 to realize, as most believe, that an historic **turning point** was reached on that very dark day.

It has ever since been accurately said, and bears repeating here, we now live in a very different world than we did on September 10, a world savagely transformed by worldwide, Islamic terrorism of historic, even biblical proportion. Recent attacks from Paris to San Bernardino to Brussels, London, and beyond bear bloody witness to this new, Dark World in which we all now reside. Without even trying to sound alarmist, I cannot help but use the term *crisis* to describe our times. Taken from the Latin term *discrimen,* the literal meaning of this important word, as noted above, is "turning point," or more directly, a "decisive moment," when the world and its peoples face unprecedented dangers on every side (Cicero, 1892).

This book, therefore, is about a specific and limited number of **signs of our times** which portend the most astounding events the world shall ever witness and experience – not the least of which will be the indescribably dramatic, thunderous Return of Jesus Christ to the earth after a personal absence of nearly 2,000 years. I have waited over 30 years to write these words, during which time I have studied and taught as a university professor in such areas as public policy, communication theory and philosophy, public affairs journalism, political communication, leadership studies, conflict resolution, cultural analysis, and comparative worldview studies.

In my more than 70 years on this planet, I have observed and experienced much to convince me the Messiah's Coming is now very, very near, and it was high time I write this book. As mentioned earlier, while I pondered completing a manuscript I began to draft in 2008, I had a strong sense on the morning of May 17, 2015, I was to finish this work by year's end. After struggling for years to write it, the words seemed to flow to completion precisely 90 days later on August 17, at which time the hard work of revising and updating the text began.

As such, I remain neither pessimistic nor optimistic about our world, but, rather, *realistic*. That is where wisdom is found, in my view – in the accurate appraisal of our world and its events, in order to understand the times from a rich and enduring biblical perspective. This was the case for those Jewish Sons of Issachar who were so insightful about their times that they were privileged to instruct all Israel what they should do to both survive and to succeed in their own perilous era (1 Chr. 12:32).

My deepest concern in this work is not, by the way, so much with the state of the world and the nation as much as it is with the *state of the Church* in America. By this term, I refer to those who genuinely believe in and follow the teachings of the God of the Bible. Fundamental to my argument here is that the nation is no better or worse than the state of its Church, as eloquently proposed by the French scholar, Alexis de Toqueville in his classic, Democracy in America. By that measure, America is not doing well because *we* are not doing well (1835).

Highly regarded survey researcher Dr. George Barna, for example, published a stunning survey on December 3, 2003 which found that only nine percent of born-again Christians possess a Biblical worldview. Deeply troubling still was his finding in July of 2014 that less than ten percent of our pastors are apparently willing to relate Scripture to "controversial" issues and threatening events occurring outside the very walls of our churches (Woodward, 2014). This, therefore, gives me grave concern over three abilities required of successful biblical living in our times: first, the ability to effectively understand the times in which we live; second, the consequent ability to make a real difference in our culture by addressing those times; and third, the ability to recognize the particular signs which herald Christ's Return.

It is my fervent hope that this brief treatment of so vast a subject matter can aid the true body of believers in the God of Scripture in her own return to *an informed faith,* which can lead others to the truth and point our culture in a much healthier direction, while there is still a little time to do so, to be found both ready and eagerly working in His fields when He does come back to us. If I succeed only a bit in this important endeavor, I shall be truly grateful to that same Lord on whom I wholly depend, as I set out on this course to help prepare the people of God – and all who will listen – for the Second Coming of the biblical Messiah to redeem the earth from its wickedness and pain.

WHAT TIME IS IT?

It has already been proposed we live in a time of intense and increasing crisis and growing danger. Most of us experience this fact in very personal ways. The rapid pace of life. Stress surrounding us on every side. The feeling that things in our lives and in the nation and the world are out of control, a sense you can find confirmed virtually anywhere you care to look.

Inexplicably crazy natural, political, and weather events. An economy that appears to be at times on the verge of collapse with debt ceilings penetrating many trillions of dollars. Gasoline and oil prices moving up and down a scale seemingly known only by the economic powers that be. A youth culture increasingly bent on pushing traditional rules of civility as far as possible. Political, racial, class, and gender divides that make the 1960s look like child's play. A pervading sense of loneliness among many of us, including Christians, even though we are surrounded by multitudes of people we call "friends" on our Facebook sites. Burgeoning military threats, ambush murders, and especially, again, Islamic terrorism spreading like a worldwide wildfire in news report after news report, as our borders crumble before our very eyes.

Underneath it all, the Old Ways, which for millennia defined moral frameworks that held us back from cultural collapse, are now being viciously challenged and laid waste more and more on a staggering scale. Thus, the drumbeat of decline and dissolution goes on everywhere, it seems; a claim thoroughly documented in the review of culture which follows.

This is the milieu into which this book is cast. In that spirit, a growing number of scholars and cultural analysts since the 1990s have begun to uncover the nature of the roots of these problems, and a few of them speak to us in the following paragraphs. Professor James Hunter of the University of

Virginia, for example, argued some time ago, "America is in the midst of a culture war that has and will continue to have reverberations not only within public policy, but within the lives of ordinary Americans everywhere ... At stake is how we as Americans will order our lives together" (1991, p. 34).

Christian intellectual Ravi Zacharias similarly warned in his compelling book, Deliver Us from Evil (1998), that "The ideas we now popularly espouse are reshaping our culture, redefining our destiny, and are at the heart of the rampant evil that we now witness ... Here we will understand the real nature of a culture in the midst of a revolution, a culture plagued with what we now call the mystery of wickedness" (p. xv).

Charles Colson, who founded Prison Fellowship Ministries, writes in his prescient book published in 1989, Against the Night, that America and the world cultures are entering upon another "Dark Age" into which, in the words of the late Christian theologian, Carl F. H. Henry, "The barbarians are coming. The Lord Jesus Christ is coming. Let the church that is here come now with Good News, with the only durable Good News, and come in time!" (Colson & Vaughn, 1989, pp. 9, 13).

And Samuel P. Huntington strikes at the center of much of this worldwide culture war in warning us there is, as captured in the title of his highly regarded 1996 work, an historic Clash of Civilizations playing out all around us. Its epicenter is found in that epochal resurgence of militant Islam seeking to create a global caliphate, in which all nations, especially Christian and Jewish ones, will bow their collective knees to mighty Allah.

Then, place on top of all of this the rivers of pornography and violence and other forms of amusement spilling out of our media, saturating entire people groups who are already weary of this historic *degringolade,* as eminent historian Paul Johnson phrased it (1983, Ch. 7). To the extent that noted New York University scholar Neil Postman predicted in 1985, long before the digital information explosion, that all of us are quite literally all about the business of *Amusing Ourselves to Death.*

So why is this true? What has happened to our world to let us slide so very near to the edge of what Gertrude Himmelfarb calls *The Abyss* (1994)? Professor and cultural analyst Gene Edward Veith, Jr. perhaps has much of the answer. In a sober appraisal of American culture, he posits we are currently living in, what he calls in the title of his book, Postmodern Times (1994), in which vast numbers of people, including many if not most people of faith, no longer believe in the existence of absolute truths (p. 16).

Citing numerous statistics to bear out this claim, it becomes starkly apparent America seems to have crossed a line during the past 50 years or so, a Rubicon of sorts, since the epochal year of 1968. For the first time in all of our 400 years of history as a nascent then actual nation, Americans increasingly appear no longer to care about the difference between right and wrong, good and evil, true or false. If so, the very life of the republic is now beyond that turning point mentioned earlier, and has reached what many are calling a "tipping point."

Support for such a view comes from many quarters. Most recently, we witnessed the meteoric rise of such presidential candidates as William Jefferson Clinton, his wife Hillary Clinton, Barack Hussein Obama, Bernie Sanders and more recently, Donald J. Trump on the other side of the aisle. Each one in his or her own way tells us much of our collective willingness to engage in serious compromise of historic principles in order to elect someone who is wildly radical by most standards, arguably unprincipled, savagely ambitious, grossly inexperienced and unqualified, or bent so low to the altar of political correctness to the point of being what Scripture would regard as fatally "lukewarm" (cf. Rev. 3:16).

In 1999, for example, William Bennett summed up this culture-wide attitude of indifference to moral order by referring to the Bill Clinton years in his incisive book as, The Absence of Outrage. Dr. James Dobson of Focus on the Family wrote similarly in his monthly newsletter of the fall of 1998, "We are facing a profound moral crisis … because our people no longer recognize the nature of evil. And when a nation reaches that state of depravity – judgment is a certainty" (2016, p. 7). David Wilkerson, in that same year, expressed, "I believe that every praying Christian and thinking American knows intuitively our nation has crossed a line of some kind – that God's patience is near an end, and a day of reckoning has come" (1998, p. 7).

Much more recently, a number of scholars have confirmed these earlier prognostications and warnings were all too accurate. One of those is from the fiery pen of Dr. Robert Jeffress, pastor of the 11,000 member First Baptist Church in Dallas, Texas, and a former Fox News contributor and news analyst. He reviews no fewer than 11 harbingers of "terrible times" hallmarked by a descent into raw Paganism, including no-fault divorce; a "birth-dearth" from disrespect for parenthood; meaningless marriage rites; defamation of past heroes; acceptance of alternative marriage forms; rapid proliferation of feminism; narcissism and hedonism; propagation of anti-family sentiment; acceptance of most forms of adultery; rebellious children; and common practice of all forms of sexual perversion (2015, pp. 79-80).

Jeffress later concludes his last chapter with this: "The moral disorder we see all around us is one of the predicted signs of *the last days*. Although I am not a prophet, you don't need to be a prophet to say this: things are bound to get worse before they get better. Carl Henry was right: 'The benign face of humanism has been ripped off so that now we see what society looks like when a nation turns away from God'" (p. 100). Indeed we do.

Thus, this book is an earnest search for the signature of the God of Abraham, Isaac, Jacob, and Yeshua ben Yosef, or Jesus of Nazareth, who foretold of the key signs of His Second Advent. It is written for the sake of His Church, all the nations, and most especially, I think, for our children.

WHAT THEN SHALL WE DO?

Extraordinary times like these demand extraordinary, exceptional wisdom. Once again, we are reminded of those desert-dusted Sons of Issachar who were remarkably insightful about their era and were, therefore, in a maximal position to instruct Israel what to do about it. Our first charge, then, is to *understand* what God says about our times. The Apostle Paul's second letter to Timothy, written from his Roman prison cell and alluded to earlier, almost brutally describes them for us:

> But realize this, that in the last days difficult times will come. For men will be lovers of self, lovers of money, boastful, arrogant, revilers, disobedient to parents, ungrateful, unholy, unloving, irreconcilable, malicious gossips, without self-control, brutal, haters of good, treacherous, reckless, conceited, lovers of pleasure rather than lovers of God; holding to a form of godliness, although they have denied its power; and avoid such men as these. For among them are those who enter into households and captivate weak women weighed down with sins, led on by various impulses, always learning and never able to come to the knowledge of the truth. (2 Tim. 3:1-7)

And there lies the epicenter of the crisis of our time: *a crisis of the truth.* Or, as the prophet Isaiah portended, "And justice is turned back, and righteousness stands far away; For truth has stumbled in the street, and uprightness cannot enter" (59:14). Jesus spent great effort in communicating that it would be this way in such a time as this, when the world would forsake truth on a massive scale, that His Coming would become fully imminent (cf., Mt. 24; Mk. 13; Lk. 21).

So, what can we then do indeed, given these dour prophecies of increasingly dark times? Do we just throw up our hands in despair and give up? We dare not! The Messiah Himself spoke to this sharply when He commanded, "We must work the works of Him who sent Me, as long as it is day; night is coming, when no man can work" (Jn. 9:4). He also warned we are to always be vigilant: "Be on the alert then, for you do not know the day nor the hour" of God's Second Advent (Mt. 25:13). Clearly, the Lord was vitally concerned that we not give up, as He further urged us to "Do business with this until I come back" (Lk. 19:13).

But do business with what? With the work He has given each of us to do, usually found in one of two Great Commissions: The first, called The Great Commission, is to share the hope and good news of the Gospel of Jesus Christ with all who will listen, and thereby "make disciples of all the nations" (Mt. 28:19-20). The second, most often called The Cultural Commission, means to become salt and light to our culture in order to preserve that which is good, and admonish that which is evil (cf. Gen. 1:26-28, Mt. 6:13-16, 19-20; also Creech, 2013).

As those first disciples asked 2,000 years ago, I am persuaded to ask once more, "Tell us, [Lord], when will these things be, and what will be *the sign* of Your coming, and of the end of the age?" (Mt. 24:3; emph. added). My purpose, in this deeply personal yet well-studied work, is to squarely address that massive question and share with you what over 30 years has taught me about those signs, *signatures* if you will, of what I am convinced is His now-imminent Return.

In fact, I will dare to be very specific: I intend to clearly identify **six such signs** I believe with all my heart and mind and spirit will immediately precede Christ's Return to Earth, the institution of what essential doctrine calls The Day of the Lord, and the gathering up of His saints to be with Him in the clouds. If I am correct, we may well be living not only in the most interesting of times, but in the most astounding time in all of human history. A time when all the various laws of Man and Nature will be torn asunder when these epic Events explode upon the entire world.

Chapter 2: The Beginning of Last Things

One of the most informative books of the Bible, concerning what is commonly referred to as "the last days" or "last things," is the Book of Daniel (c. 605 BC - 533 BC). In chapter 12, verse one of this gifted Jewish prophet's writings, we find a rich context into which to cast our introductory remarks for this study:

> Now at that time Michael, the great prince who stands guard over the sons of your people, will arise. And there will be *a time of distress* such as never occurred since there was a nation until that time; and at that time your people, everyone who is found written in the book, will be rescued. (emph. added)

The key phrase here is the reference to "a time of distress." Theologian William Barclay elaborates on this under the aegis of "The Apparatus of Apocalyptic" (1959, p. 7). This period of history, or "the end times," is characterized by a series of events and characteristics. What follows is a partial summary of those aspects of things that occur in the end of history as we know it, according to Barclay.

In this apocalyptic era, first the Jewish Messiah is viewed as the central, all-powerful figure who waits to descend into the middle of earth's intensifying tribulations to announce He is, in effect, taking complete control over them in order to set the world aright once more. Second, the coming of the Messiah will be preceded by the return of Elijah, or more figuratively the spirit of Elijah, who would prepare the way for His Return. Third, these last times are known as, among other things, "the travail of the Messiah" (Barclay, 1959, p. 8). It is likened to the agony of birth – a key point in this present study. Fourth, the end times will be a time of enormous, worldwide terror, in which the strongest of men will tremble and run for cover wherever they might find it. Fifth, this era will also be a time when the entire world is quite literally shattered, with the very earth and heavens heaving to and fro out of their normal emplacements. Sixth, human relationships will subsequently suffer greatly, as hatred and conflict will characterize even family and ethnic groups. Seventh, clearly the last day will be a time of judgment, in which God will come as an Avenger to all evildoers. And eighth, Jews will increasingly return from throughout the earth to their historic homeland of Israel.

An important distinction here is, beyond a shadow of any doubt, this period of time will increasingly be both characterized by and known as **A Time of Divine Wrath.** This is particularly important to this work, since further distinction must be made between two primary sources of wrath: (1) Satan's wrath and (2) God's Wrath. Each type stands in cataclysmic contrast to the other, as the earth and its peoples reel back and forth while both God and Satan make their presence known in the most apocalyptic terms. As we will see later in this work, our principal concern here will be with the approach of God's Wrath and the crucial underlying presupposition that *God's people are not appointed to His Wrath,* but are not immune from Satan's wrath.

Scripture is lucid on this vital point: "For God has not destined us for [His] wrath, but for obtaining salvation through our Lord Jesus Christ" (1 Thess. 5:9). And to the church at Philadelphia, John writes the very words of Christ on the matter: "Because you have kept the word of My perseverance, I also will keep you from the hour of testing, that hour which is about to come upon the whole world, to test those who dwell upon the earth" (Rev. 3:10). Clearly and consistently then, God's people of The Book are not required to endure the unremitting Wrath of their God.

However, it is a major proposition of this analysis that all people, including the Lord's, cannot avoid a portion of Satan's wrath. An operational definition of where that wrath is to be found is in the *strong parallels* existing between Christ's famous

Olivet Discourse (again, Matt. 24; Mk. 13; Lk. 21) and the sixth chapter of Revelation. It is my considered view that the Body of Christ is, in fact, appointed to remain here on earth throughout the pouring forth of those birth pangs described in these passages (e.g., Mt. 24:8). This represents a substantial but not radical rethinking of the traditional Premillennial, Pre-tribulational, and more recently, "Pre-wrath" positions, described a bit later in this chapter. Indeed, it is one of my central purposes to reconcile these three traditions.

The primary consideration here is God's people don't get a free pass from trouble during this period of history, on the one hand, as Satan does his level best to bring chaos to the earth. On the other, we are kept from the expression of God's Great Anger on the earth, since it is reserved only for the enemies of God (cf. Na. 1:2). Much more will be said of this as we study more deeply the subject of Christ's Second Coming throughout this work.

ON STUDYING THE BOOK OF REVELATION

Several preliminary considerations must precede any intensive examination of the Book of Revelation. First, of course, concerns authorship. There is overwhelming historical consensus the apostle John was its author, as Christ revealed its contents to him on the Greek Isle of Patmos in or around the last decade of the first century, during the reign of the Emperor Domitian (A.D. 81-96; Ladd, 1972, pp. 7-8). The title of this enigmatic book translates from the Greek, *apokalupsis,* as in, "to take the cover off," or an "uncovering" of, in Zodhiates' terms, "the glory of Christ and of what the future holds" (1990, p. 1671). This meaning, in turn, reminds us of Daniel 12 again: "But as for you, Daniel, conceal these words and seal up the book until the end of time; many will go back and forth, and *knowledge will increase*" (v. 4; emph. added). There is in this the implicit notion that it would only be at the end of time when the Lord would reopen prophetic Scripture for further and deeper understanding. I firmly believe we are in such a time.

As many readers may already know, there are four classical schools of interpretation regarding the Book of Revelation. The *Preterist* view argues the events of the book already took place largely during the first century mentioned above, relegating the entire book to the realm of symbolism found in the remote past. Given the clearly prophetic nature of Revelation, this view is quite inadequate to the proper understanding of its contents.

A second view is the historical or *Historicist* perspective, in which still another symbolic theory is advanced. This time, however, the interpreter believes Revelation covers the vast sweep of human history, from the first century to the Second Coming of Christ and the end of the age. Popular among many of the Protestant Reformers, this approach viewed the Roman Church as the enemy of Christ and became for the longest time the Protestant theology of the end times (cf. Ladd, 1972, p. 11; Zodhiates, 1990, p. 1671). Its attempt to coordinate historical events with the various visions of Revelation is seen by most Biblical scholars as highly arbitrary at best, and inadequate interpretation at worst.

The third school of thought is called the symbolic or *Idealist* view which proposes still another allegorical perspective, in which the book describes the cosmic conflict between God's good and Satan's evil throughout history. Unlike the Historicist view, however, it does not attempt to link the contents of Revelation with specific, earth-bound events as it, too, views the contents of this important book irrelevant to understanding real history, or real events occurring in the world.

Once again, the intensively apocalyptic nature of the book argues forcefully against this view, so we must look further to what is called the *Futurist* perspective, the only one assuming a more literal and truly prophetic view of this important, clearly prophetic book. While it recognizes the often symbolic nature of Revelation, it gives proper ground to literalist interpretation when the content calls for it. From chapter 4 on, this view and my own hold the Book of Revelation as a detailed, roughly chronological, and dramatic portrayal of the times just preceding, accompanying, and following the Return of the Messiah to judge the earth.

As stated earlier, our study will concern itself primarily with **the sixth chapter of Revelation** as its central focus, which unapologetically takes the Futurist approach. In a substantial but not radical departure from the traditional views of Revelation described earlier (i.e., the Premillennial, Pre-tribulational), this analysis presupposes chapter 1 of Revelation deals with the past. Chapters 2 and 3 tell us about the things and events that were taking place during John's stay on Patmos. Chapters 4 and 5 portray the events in Heaven, occurring in what I believe to be roughly *the present hour*, as the heavenly host observe Christ making ready to open the first of seven seals beginning in chapter 6.

Importantly, chapter 6, therefore, describes events in perfect harmony with the Olivet Discourse, in which Jesus outlines the numerous signs that will appear just before His Second Coming. It is my strong conviction that those seals have already begun to be opened by our Lord, and we are thus catapulting into the throes of final birth pangs before the onset of God's fiery Wrath, which commences in full following chapter 7's sealing of the 144,000 Jews who will, from chapter 8 onward, serve as earth's evangelists during the darkest times of the Great Tribulation.

If I am correct in these preliminary proposals, we are so very near indeed to the Messiah's Second Coming that one is cautioned to hear once again the stirring words of our Lord as recorded in Luke 21:36: "But keep on the alert at all times, praying in order that you may have strength to escape all these things that are about to take place, and to stand before the Son of Man."

Dear reader, it is my fervent, if not furious, belief we have already entered that narrow birth canal described collectively in Matthew 24, Mark 13, Luke 21, and Revelation 6, which will lead more and more rapidly to that Day of days, the Day of the Lord. That day commences when He comes with His winnowing fork in hand, as He prepares to thoroughly clear out His threshing floor and gather His wheat into the barn to burn up with "unquenchable fire" all the chaff of the earth (Mt. 3:12). But please note again Jesus promises the obedient servant that while he will face Satan's early angers, he will yet be privileged to *escape* (*ekpheugo,* "flee away out of") the Great Tribulation which commences with chapter 8.

Finally, to adequately prepare for our journey into these Days of Awe, as many Jews term them, we must briefly consider the various Millennial views surrounding the study of the Book of Revelation. I borrow considerably here from the Holman New Testament Commentary on the Book of Revelation edited by Easley and Anders (2007, pp. 4-8). **Millennialism** finds its origin in Revelation 20:1-6, only a portion of which is reproduced here:

> And I saw an angel coming down from heaven, having the key of the abyss and a great chain in his hand. And he laid hold of the dragon, the serpent of old, who is the devil and Satan, and bound him for *a thousand years*, and threw him into the abyss, and shut it and sealed it over him, so that he should not deceive the nations any longer, until the thousand years were completed; after these things he must be released for a short time. (vv. 1-3; emph. added)

While our present concern is not with why he is released for a short time after the Millennial time, it is important to recognize schools of interpretation have emerged over whether or not the "thousand years" is symbolic or literal.

The first is called *Amillennialism* (or 'no millennium') which holds the highly symbolic view that evil continues to persist on the earth, believers simply ascend to Heaven at death to be with the Lord, and remain there to reign with Him for a symbolic length of time noted as the 1,000 years. Christians remaining on the earth will experience Great Tribulation and be raptured (or raised) at its end. More detail on the doctrine of The Rapture is presented later in this work. This view rejects a chronological and literal definition of the Millennium. Thus, this position constitutes an "Amillennial, Post-tribulational" perspective.

A second view is called *Postmillennialism,* in which tribulation includes a long, unspecified period of time on earth, followed by a powerful missions outreach which engenders a Golden Age (i.e., Millennium) of a symbolic 1,000 years, after which Christ returns visibly, people either go to Heaven or Hell, and eternity continues on forever in both cases. This view is held most recently in Christian Reconstructionism, founded by R.J. Rushdoony (Rogers, 2008). In this Triumphalist view, sometimes associated with Replacement Theology which argues that Jewish Israel is replaced by the Church, Christians are empowered by God to bring a virtual utopia to the earth, so Christ may return (cf. Acts 3:19-21). Thus, Christians will experience Great Tribulation while on earth, preceding that Golden Age on earth, after which they will be raptured to be with the Lord forever. Consequently, this view constitutes a "Postmillennial, Post-tribulational" perspective.

To drill down a bit more on this terribly important topic, described by most experts as this increasingly influential theological movement: "Most of the contemporary movements labeled Dominion Theology or Dominionism arose in the 1970s in religious movements reasserting aspects of Christian nationalism. Ideas for how to accomplish this vary. Very doctrinaire versions of Dominion Theology are sometimes called Hard Dominionism or Theocratic Dominionism, because they seek relatively authoritarian theocratic or theonomic forms of government" (Dominion Theology, 2015; also see House & Ice, 1988).

It is vital to note the darkest contours of this line of heterodoxy (i.e., an unreliable blend of orthodox and unorthodox doctrine) lead to an incipient anti-Zionism and more deeply, anti-Semitism, and injures the very heart and soul of biblical prophecy in my studied view. Thus warranting the special attention paid to it. It is also to be found in the present day calls around the world, and especially here in the United States, for a New Nationalism of sorts, as with the rise of an Alt-Right movement of the kind found in the fervent "Make America Great Again" narrative led by Donald J. Trump, with its emphasis on super patriotism, economic hegemony, and political pragmatism (Buchanan, 2015).

Finally, there are two types of *Premillennialism.* Historic Premillennialism involves the evil on earth becoming more and more widespread with many Christians being persecuted and martyred during a seven-year period of Great Tribulation. Following this time, Christ will return to rapture the Church after they have endured great trials, thus commencing the institution of the Millennial time. Therefore, this approach constitutes a Premillennial, Post-tribulational perspective.

The second type is referred to as Dispensational Premillennialism, in which history is divided into either three or seven dispensations or covenants with God, requiring different responsibilities to God from His people. Before evil reaches its most wicked intensity, believers are lifted out of, or raptured (see Prasch, 2014), from the earth's travails, constituting a "Premillennial, Pre-tribulational" perspective. There is also a third view held by a minority that might be labeled "Premillennial, Mid-tribulational," in which Christians are to experience only the first half of the Great Tribulation, but not its most intense second half.

APPROACH TO THE COMMENTARY

For all intents and purposes, the approach taken here may be most specifically described as a **Post-Seal, Pre-Wrath, Premillennial, Pre-Tribulational** perspective. I know, it's complicated. But put simply, this means several things: (1) Believers are *not* going to go through the Great Tribulation of seven years prophesied in Daniel 9:24-27, which I define here as God's Wrath. (2) Believers *are* going to face the beginnings of Satan's end time wrath defined by the birth pangs found in the Olivet Discourse and Revelation 6. (3) Believers will be in Heaven with the Lord during the seven years of Great Tribulation, preparing for a return to earth with Christ to reign with Him for a literal, 1,000 period. After the events of the Millennium come to an end, we will enter Eternity with the Lord to co-reign with Him throughout the recreated universe forever and ever. Selah.

All of this, even in such a brief treatment, is a great deal to comprehend. For the purposes of this commentary, the reader will be directed most intensely, again, to the sixth chapter of Revelation. In doing so, I stand in agreement with Easley and Anders's statement of "Principles for Interpreting Revelation" (1999, p. 8). They include: (a) Figurative language will be taken and understood as just that, according to first-century understanding; (b) Simplicity of meaning will be the rule where Scripture's obvious and more literal meanings are displayed, as opposed to some kind of mystical, symbolic reinterpretation; (c) Chronological understanding will be assumed where, again, it is clearly the case. Without question, the entire Book of Revelation, though it jumps back and forth at times, moves from less intense to more severely intense events. As mentioned earlier, one cannot grasp the overall sense of The Apocalypse unless this rough chronology is honored wherever possible.

Finally, I remind the reader about the introduction of this overview. There is found here a commitment to the idea that things in the earth, and even above the earth, are getting worse and worse, not better and better. In dramatic contrast to the various Triumphalist Models emerging today, the entire notion of *historical decline* found here is not unlike that set forth by respected historian, philosopher, theologian, and barrister John Warwick Montgomery (1986) in his many works which collectively reject the notion of any sort of historic utopianism.

Lest you bridle at this important presuppositional hermeneutic, I remind you it was *Christ Himself*, after all, who made it unequivocally clear the end of history would be characterized by such decline, even to the point where He fervently warned: "And at that time many will fall away and will deliver up one another and hate one another ... And because *lawlessness is increased*, most people's love will grow cold" (Mt. 24:10, 12; emph. added). Unmistakable, undeniable, and chilling words indeed.

So let us be forewarned: This analysis will not attempt to soften the severity of our times; neither will it need to enlarge it. They stand on their own witness as times of great and increasing distress, and we, as God's people, are to be uniformly educated about them, that we might warn others of what is coming, to bring them to rescue in Christ and His Church. As Jesus said so clearly to us all, *real wisdom is knowing what is to come,* and thereby, knowing what to do about it (cf. Jn. 16:13).

Chapter 3: The First Seal Judgment

Thus, do we now embark on a rather stupendous biblical journey, as we open the first great seal of **the sixth chapter of Revelation**, the force and focus of the present analysis. Easley and Anders (1999) again remind us that the disciples in Matthew 24-25, Mark 13, and Luke 21 asked for *the sign* heralding Christ's Coming and the end of the age (cf. Mt. 24:3). But rather than giving them a direct answer to their pointed question, Jesus decided to give them a list of several signs that would serve as epochal Prelude to His Return.

The Olivet Discourse runs a close parallel to the events described in Revelation 6 – no small point to this study. While chapters 4 and 5 of Revelation refer clearly to events in Heaven, chapter 6 begins to transition us from that scene to events that, as I have argued here, are already beginning to occur upon the earth – and in some cases, above, and even beneath, the earth. Most traditional treatments of these events presuppose they constitute the beginning of what is known as The Great Tribulation, commensurate with the spilling forth of God's Wrath.

Again, that is not the case with this analysis. To restate it: A close examination of both the Olivet Discourse and Revelation 6 reveals these are, in theological fact, merely **the beginning of sorrows,** as the Aramaic renders it, or preliminary stepping stones to the later onset of God's subsequent, all-encompassing Wrath. In Christ's very own words, "But all these things are *merely* the beginning of birth pangs." (Mt. 24:8) The word *merely* in the original text is significant to the context here, as with the vernacular, "Hey! This isn't the Big One, *only* the warmup period." Or thoughts to that effect. I have come to view these birth pangs, therefore, as the onset of the combination of Man's great folly and Satan's end-time wrath, since none of the first five seals describe supernatural events as much as an intensifying of relatively normal, albeit devastating, occurrences upon the earth.

NOTES ON "THE BOOK" OF CHAPTER 5

Before venturing into the depths of chapter 6, however, several things must be said concerning the preliminary chapter 5. Of special note, the first verse gives us a picture of the cosmological stage that is being set before John: "And I saw in the right hand of Him who sat on the throne *a book* written inside and on the back, sealed up with seven seals" (emph. added). We first notice that the book is held in the right hand of "Him who sat on the throne," an unequivocal reference to God the Father, according to virtually all commentaries. The intense focus here is on "a book," or one might say more appropriately, *the* book, insofar as it is absolutely unique in the entire universe and contains such powerful information that only God Himself may hold it.

Several views exist as to the proper identity of this book (see Ladd's review, 1972, pp. 79-82). Of all the possibilities, there appears to be a consensus it is in substance and implication "the Book of the End" (see Hendley, 1985, p. 76). It is in the words of another source, "God's judgment scroll" for the end times (Easley and Anders, 1999, p. 1). It contains, significantly, all of the expressions of God's Wrath and Redemption, beginning in Revelation 7:1 through Revelation 22:21 (cf. Ladd, 1972, p. 81). Please also note carefully, still again, that such wrathful expression does not begin with chapter 6, but rather with chapter 8. More on this in a later chapter.

More specifically, we see that the Day of the Lord does not commence with the breaking of the first five seals, but at the very earliest, with the breaking of **the sixth seal,** the very thesis, and therefore title, of this present study. Much more of this will be written in later sections, but the reader is hereby notified that the full measure of God's Wrath will commence *after* the opening of this sixth seal, followed by the unveiling of the 144,000 Jews of chapter 7, and then a deafening silence in Heaven found in Revelation 8:1.

A final preliminary note must also be made concerning Revelation 5:2, as John stands witness to the extraordinary events continuing to take place in Heaven: "And I saw a strong angel proclaiming with a loud voice, 'Who is worthy to open the book and to break its seals?'" Later in the 4th verse, we see John weeping greatly, since apparently there was no one in Heaven, or on the earth, or under the earth (v. 3) who could open the book and break its seals. Except for One Person whom one of the "elders" pointed out to John was, in fact, worthy to do so. He said, "Stop weeping; behold, the Lion that is from the tribe of Judah, the Root of David, has overcome so as to open the book and its seven seals" (Rev. 5:5). One verse later, this Lion is regarded also as, "a Lamb standing, as if slain, having seven horns and seven eyes, which are the seven Spirits of God, sent out into all the earth."

Thus, the remainder of chapter 5 is an emphatic and dramatic pronouncement that **Jesus Christ** is the only One worthy to take the book from His Father's hand and break the seals, to both reveal and release its powerful contents. So, as all of history and heaven virtually holds its cosmic breath, the Messiah steps forth to supervise the commencement of The Consummation of that history. No more powerful moment is ever recorded in all the books of the world or universe, as in this one little book, or "scroll," more accurately. We turn now to the central purpose of this analysis and the step-by-step opening of each of the six seals of Revelation chapter 6.

OPENING OF THE FIRST SEAL

And I saw when the Lamb broke one of the seven seals, and I heard one of the four living creatures saying as with a voice of thunder, "Come." And I looked, and behold, a white horse, and he who sat on it had a bow;

and a crown was given to him; and he went out conquering, and to conquer. (Rev. 6:1-2)

As we begin our own opening of the next six seals, we will proceed by looking at each major figure, phrase, or element in each of the seal passages, in order to closely examine its primary message. It should also be noted there will be a distinction made between that which is intended to be read literally and that which is figurative or symbolic. The goal here is to capture the essential truths contained in these often enigmatic scriptures.

The Lamb

The primary focus of the entire Book of Revelation and this passage is upon Someone called, "The Lamb." In Revelation 5:6, we recall this Lamb was described as One who was "slain" or slaughtered. Previously referred to as the "Lion" of the tribe of Judah and the Root of David, this Figure was seen "standing" but who possessed the sole authority to take the Book out of the hand of God the Father and to ultimately, break its seals and open the Book. Too, He is in the center of the throne of God, the entire heavenly host, and even all created things "on the earth and under the earth and on the sea, and all things in them" (Rev. 5:11-13). In effect, the Lord's entire cosmic order is seen as passionately worshiping this Lamb. It is also important to note several distinguishing characteristics that further define this important figure.

First, as mentioned earlier, this Lamb has been at one time "slain." Second, and obviously symbolic, the Lamb has seven horns, suggestive of the fullness of divine power possessed by this individual. Third, the Lamb has seven eyes, which are described as the seven spirits of God, here symbolic of the ability for this Lamb to see and know all things. Fourth, this Lamb is the only one worthy in the entire universe to both hold and open this sacred Book. Finally, Easley and Anders point out this figure was further characterized by seven elements that round out the biblical definition of the Lamb: Power, Wealth, Wisdom, Strength, Honor, Glory, and Praise (cf. Rev. 5:9-14; Easley & Anders, 1999, pp. 92-96). The great majority of commentaries on Revelation conclude, with Ladd (1972), this Lamb is "the conquering Christ," whose scepter of perfect authority will never depart from Him (p. 83).

A Voice of Thunder

Next we see, or rather hear as it were, a "voice of thunder" emanating from one of the four living creatures surrounding the throne of God. Though it cannot be literally proved by Scripture, there is an implicit suggestion that there were some moments of silence between the closing of cosmic adoration in Revelation 5:14 and the opening of the seal in Revelation 6:1 – I have a picture in mind of this thunderous voice literally crashing through that silence loudly enough to be heard in the furthest corners of the entire universe. The command given by that voice is in a single word, "Come!" Some manuscripts add the phrase "and see," but most copyists agree that is not the most accurate rendering (Ladd, 1972, p. 96). The Greek word for *come* is *erchomai,* which in this context refers to a command of great force for something to "Go forth" or to "Arrive" (Strong, 2009). Note that this powerful command is not in fact given to John, the recorder of this astounding vision, but rather to the first of four horsemen who is about to ride from Heaven to the earth in order to render a judgment of some sort.

Thus begins **the onset of birth pangs**, according to this and several other sources (e.g., Van Kampen, 1992; Montgomery, 2008). As Van Kampen observes:

> These events [described in Revelation 6] ... correspond to Christ's description of these same events in the Olivet Discourse (see Matt. 24:4-8). Yet in the Olivet Discourse, He refers to these initial afflictions as "merely the beginning of birth pangs" (Matt. 24:8). A few verses

later, Christ explains what the "hard labor" will be: "a great tribulation, such as has not occurred since the beginning of the world until now, nor ever shall be" (v. 21). (p. 198)

Though I depart significantly from Van Kampen's analysis regarding the timing of these events, the strong point being made with which I concur is that by this reasoning, this is <u>not</u> the pouring forth of God's Wrath, but rather the beginning of a combination of man's foolishness and Satan's intensifying angers – albeit with God's approval and signature.

The reader is therefore strongly admonished to be fully prepared to experience and endure these seal judgments, since it is my clear conviction that even God's people will go fully through Christ's birth pangs. Once again, this position is regarded as a modified or revised *Post Seal, Pre-Wrath, Pre-Millennial, Pre-Tribulational* perspective on the Second Coming of the Messiah. The academic and theological question is thus thrust upon us: **When will God's Wrath appear?** The overriding purpose of this work is to unequivocally answer that question and to address the many implications of such a view. Suffice for now to remind the reader that Scripture is clear on a single point: Christ's true church will *not* be subjected to the Wrath of God (see esp. 1 Thess. 4:15-18; 5:1-11). This crucial point will be thoroughly and repeatedly explored and elaborated as we go through each of the seal judgments in the chapters ahead.

And this entire, unprecedented cosmic drama begins with what both Church and history have recorded as **The Four Horsemen of the Apocalypse**. So, let the play begin.

The White Horse

John next sees "a white horse" and a rider, moving forth following the command to "Come." Our attention for the moment is on that horse and not yet the rider. Popularly known as *the first horse* among the Four Horseman of the Apocalypse, there is some controversy over the identity of the white horse, and more specifically, if it is the same horse described in Revelation 19:11-21. According to the present view and many commentaries, those horses in Revelation 19 are literal horses with literal riders. By contrast, this white horse is highly symbolic, as are the remaining three, used here to allegorically represent a particular judgmental event that will take place in relation to the mission of both horse and rider. While some argue the color of the horse here (white) is significantly symbolic, it is not clear what that symbolism is.

The Rider

Of vastly greater importance is the proper identification of the one who rides the white horse. Again, much controversy surrounds this question, and a significant minority argue it is none other than Jesus Christ (cf. Ladd, 1972; Morris, 1983; Thames, 2014, p. 53). F. A. Jennings, however, rightly rejects this view and states: "The whole context and character of these seals absolutely forbid our thinking of this rider being the Lord Jesus, as so many affirm. His reign shall not bring war, famine, and strife in its train" (as cited in Gregg, 1997, p. 103). Or as J. M. Hendley writes, "This is not Christ, because He cannot be the One supervising from heaven during the time of the end and also be the one coming at the same time" (1985, p. 84). So if this rider is not Jesus Christ, who is he?

Most Futurists (of whom I am one) strongly agree this rider on the white horse is someone going forth "to conquer" by largely human devices (Rev. 6:2). He is given a crown and holds a bow, though no quiver of arrows is present which suggests that whoever he is, he will do his conquering in an initially discreet political, likely deceptive, manner rather than as a military man, using both conventional weapons and weapons of mass destruction. As one commentary put it, he rides forth to persuade the world into believing *he alone* has the answers to earth's problems and is capable of bringing a peaceful utopia (which means, by the way, "no place") to the world.

Easley and Anders provide a neat summary of this point:

> From the first century until today, powerful generals around the globe have set out bent on conquest, yet appearing, at least at first, as peaceable to the conquered peoples (the early days of the Third Reich come to mind). Although such a human leader may suppose he is in charge, John knew that the victor's crown was given or permitted only by God – and then only to the extent that God allows. (1999, p. 106)

The rider on this horse, then, is most likely *the Antichrist*, the man of sin. This false christ is written of throughout Scripture, and we will look at some of those verses shortly. For now, let us recognize that today this troubled planet is looking for such a leader, someone who cries out "peace and safety!" in the midst of anything but peace and safety. I cannot help but think here of the 2016 presidential primaries, during which both parties were in nearly unprecedented turmoil over who shall lead America for the next several years. On the Democrat side, there was a rising tide for the underdog Socialist Bernie Sanders, junior senator from Vermont, and the machine-like Liberal icon, Hillary Clinton, versus the controversial populist and New York real estate mogul Donald Trump for the Republicans – *All* of whom would promise to be strong Statists in the image of President Barack Obama, in order to restore the American order.

And not one of them a true biblical conservative, a political and theological reality of potentially historic proportion. President Trump now the presumed political savior of the Republic appears more and more like an authoritarian statist.

While each of these unlikely competitors for the presidential throne of almost unlimited power are viewed as human messiahs of sorts, we find in 1 Thessalonians 5:2-3,

"For you yourselves know full well that the day of the Lord will come just like a thief in the night. While they are saying, 'peace and safety!' then destruction will come upon them suddenly like birth pangs upon a woman with child; and they shall not escape." Thus, it is possible this leader will ride the crest of a worldwide pacifist-isolationist movement on the one hand, or a nationalist-supremacist movement on the other, not unlike the stark contrasts served up by Neville Chamberlain's appeasement policies in Great Britain versus Adolf Hitler's savage German Fascism of the 1930s.

In any case, the Olivet Discourse warns us of such men arising on the scene during the Last Days. "For false Christs and false prophets will arise and will show great signs and wonders, so as to mislead, if possible, *even the elect*" (Matt. 24:24; emph. added). And earlier in that same address, the very real Christ strongly warns: "See to it that no one misleads you. For many will come in My name, saying, 'I am the Christ,' and will mislead many" (Matt. 24:4-5). Thus, it is suggested this man of sin will be able to beguile people of the earth and even the Church with his powerful and sensational rhetoric, handsome appearance, noble-sounding causes, passionate arguments, and very likely promise to bring people into worldwide unity, further suggestive of a utopian kingdom here on earth.

Sadly, tragically, many who are not grounded in the truths of God and Scripture and affirmed by His Spirit will believe him during this era of increasing, worldwide deception brought on by the catastrophic loss of the traditional moral frameworks detailed in the earlier chapters. As Jesus passionately proclaimed the consequences of such a time: "And at that time *many will fall away* and will deliver up one another and hate one another," as a spirit of massive, divisive falsehood and delusion descend upon the entire planet under his spell (Matt. 24:10-11; emph. added). The fruit of this period of time will be characterized by **chaos and division** on an unprecedented scale.

On a more personal note, I am becoming more and more convinced the false christs who precede the Antichrist and the Antichrist himself will not be the ones who appear obviously false to many of our citizens. Rather, they very possibly are (or claim to be) members of a respected church congregation who speak the language of the church convincingly and generally look and sound like Christians yet corrupt the words of God just enough to render them false, but not so much as to convince others they are not representative of the truth.

My strong suspicion is many of these faux teachers and leaders will be advocates of what I call the "Love Only" movement in the Church, usually associated with the more liberal, social gospel wing of Christianity. Here the idea is God's Love and *Tolerance for All* is the only answer to world ills, naively at the staggering price of Truth (see Balogh, 2013; Wallis, 2015). Thus does Francis Schaeffer's Spirit of Accommodation to the world spirit become the ensign of our times, as he proclaimed in his last book before his death, The Great Evangelical Disaster (1984).

This is why it is so terribly vital that believers develop and nurture a richly biblical worldview in the Last Days, which, according to that astounding study by George Barna, is clearly not the case (2003). As noted before, he found that no more than 9 percent of the Body of Christ exhibited such a view, a clear and present danger to the other 91 percent who may not have a clue when Antichrist forms his powerful arguments to follow him. And his later finding that about 90 percent of American pastors refuse to teach on such issues facing the nation as abortion, Islamic Jihad, and the gay marriage movement, in order to preserve their financial base for church programs, expansion, and everyday expenses (Leclaire, 2014). Truly unfathomable.

Most recently, a new train of thought has arisen arguing for the possibility of a Muslim Antichrist. Joel Richardson, for example, constructs an intriguing yet troubling parallel between the Antichrist and an Islamic personage called the "Mahdi," the Muslim conception of the awaited messiah who will come to defeat the forces aligned against Islam once and for all (2006; see Ch. 4). In similar fashion, two other books suggest that this Mahdi – the Muslim messiah – could well be the Christian's Antichrist in a cunning reversal of roles and titles regarding the End Times (cf. Williams, 2007; Stice, 2005). While these ideas are untested by rigorous theological analysis, they are mentioned here to open up our understanding of the colossal historic impact Islamic extremism is having on today's troubled world.

That being said, an in-depth treatment of the rise of Antichrist will not be presented here, but the reader may consult several other sources for such detail (e.g., Hendley, 1985, Ch. 13; Montaigne, 2014). Yet it is important to note that by this analysis, the Antichrist is presumed to be presently alive today, though his identity will not be fully revealed until the body of believers in Christ (who carry the Holy Spirit) is removed by the divine Removal of the church from the earth. Scripture clarifies this crucial point: "And you know what restrains him now, so that in his time he may be revealed. For the mystery of lawlessness is already at work; only [He] who now restrains will do so until [He] is taken out of the way. And then that lawless one will be revealed whom the Lord will slay with the breath of His mouth and bring to an end by the appearance of His coming" (2 Thess. 2:6-8; cf. 2 Tim. 4:8; NKJV rendering of *He*).

The most obvious application here is that while we ought to be about the business of developing our biblical worldview and ability for discerning truth from falsehood, we need not concern ourselves with identifying who the Antichrist will be. Rather, we are to remain vigilant for the arrival of that *spirit* of Antichrist which is prevalent in today's world at many levels. Even more importantly, we must remain on the alert for the signs which will herald the Coming of the Jewish-Christian Messiah, Jesus Christ, thereby following in the tradition of the Sons of Issachar mentioned earlier who studied and therefore knew the times in which they lived. Thus a brief consideration of the development of a Christian worldview is offered as proper response to the charge to refine our ability for Understanding the Times, the very title of a well-known book by Dr. David Noebel (1994).

THE IMPORTANCE OF A CHRISTIAN WORLDVIEW

Although the concept of worldview has been around for centuries, it is only during the past 40 years or so that the term has received considerable attention in Christian academic circles. Professor David Naugle of Dallas Baptist University, for example, traces the history of the concept's development and begins by quoting Richard Weaver who prophetically wrote, "world view is the most important thing about a man, because, among other things, it reveals what he believes, or does not believe, about the existence of universals. And that tells us whether or not he accepts or denies the existence of truth itself" (2002, p. xi; cf. Weaver, 1948, p. 4). I have already argued that we live in an age that increasingly denies absolute Truth and eagerly replaces it with a collection of preferred fictions or myths.

In order to understand the titanic struggle over which worldviews will dominate the 21st century, it is important to first define the concept. Charles Colson offers us a concise definition in his excellent book, How Now Shall We Live? (1999). He writes, "It is simply the sum total of our beliefs about the world, the 'big picture' that directs our daily decisions and actions" (p. 14). So a worldview's major function, as alluded to above, is to determine for us what is true and what is false, what is good and what is evil, and what is, as a consequence, the very best way to order our lives. Obviously, it is a terribly important concept since it has the effect of explaining all human behavior, whether at the individual actor level, or more collectively at the societal and political levels.

Based on the available and rapidly growing worldview literature, I have over the years outlined several classic worldview perspectives that compete for a culture's attention. Drawing heavily upon the thorough research conducted by James Sire in The Universe Next Door (2009), I have created a simple taxonomy of **Four Worldview Systems** that help us to understand the times in which we now live. We will briefly review each one and conclude with a brief commentary on the state of the American church in relation to the worldview issue.

James Sire's widely influential work then provides the presuppositional benchmarks for the four worldviews which follow. The first of them, what I will call *Judeo-Christian Theism,* begins with a stated belief in God as the infinite and personal (triune), transcendent and immanent, omniscient, sovereign and ultimate good. Second, that same God created the cosmos *ex nihilo* (or *from nothing*) to operate with a uniformity of cause and effect in an open system. Third, human beings are created in His image and thus possess personality, self-transcendence, intelligence, morality, gregariousness and creativity. Fourth, humans can know God and the world He created because man was given the ability for cognitive understanding and a language through which he can commune and communicate with His Creator. Fifth, human beings were created good, but through a catastrophic Fall, the image of God was defaced but through the work of Christ, God redeemed humanity and began the long process of redemption from original sin. Sixth, all men die but will live eternally in the presence of God in Heaven or eternally separate from God in Hell. Seventh, ethics are transcendent and based on the character of God as good, holy and loving. Finally, history is linear, meaningful and sequential in nature and is filled with events leading to an Eschaton, or perfected fulfillment of God's purposes for humanity and the entire universe (Sire, 2009, pp. 23-36).

The second worldview I have labeled, *Classical Deism.* In this framework, God is regarded not so much as a Person as a First Cause who created all things, then left it to run according to immutable laws and principles. He is thus no longer immanent, sovereign, or providential over human affairs. Second, the cosmos God created is determined as a uniformity of cause and effect in a closed system and therefore no miracles are possible. Third, human beings, though personal, are a part of a massive clockwork universe and as such have no personal relationship to or commerce with God. Fourth, the created universe is regarded as normal and not fallen, and we can know that universe and its Creator to some extent by studying it. Fifth, ethics is limited to general revelation; because the universe is normal, it reveals what is right. To restate it in somewhat startling terms, "whatever is, is right" (Sire, 2009, pp. 43-48). For the record, most authorities place Islam somewhere within the Deistic framework because Islamic conceptions of God or Allah closely resemble a rather dark version of the God of Deism (Nash, 1992, pp. 36-37).

A third worldview perspective, and one which I regard as presently dominant in the world's major institutions today, is what I term *Atheistic Naturalism.* Wisely pointing out that Deism serves as an "isthmus" to Naturalism, Sire begins to describe this third worldview as one in which matter exists eternally, and is all there is; God does not exist. Second, the cosmos exists again as a uniformity of cause and effect in a completely closed system; there is nothing *out there* that is transcendent. Third, humans are nothing more than complex machines, a combination of chemical and physical properties we do not yet fully understand. Fourth, death is simply the extinction of personality, individuality and being, period. There is no afterlife. Fifth, history is a stream of linear events linked by cause and effect, with no overarching purpose. The ultimate implication of this kind of thought is that truth is either non-existent or irrelevant and thus personally defined; therefore, human existence has no particular meaning outside of one's own construction of it (cf. Delia, O'Keefe & O'Keefe 1982).

Finally, there is something I call *Pagan Mysticism* – a potpourri of largely Eastern religious conceptions of reality usually known as the New Age Worldview. Its presuppositions are so obfuscated, that what follows will likely confuse the reader as much as it does its adherents! Nonetheless, here we go.

First, whatever its definition of the nature of being, the Self is central – the "prime reality" – and there is an underlying assumption that something transformative is about to take place which will result in all Selfs within humanity reaching a heightened state of unified existence in this utopian New Age. Second, the cosmos while unified in the all-important Self, is accessible through altered states of consciousness, whether through meditation or chemically assisted inducements. Third, the core experience therefore is something called "cosmic consciousness," in which ordinary categories of space, time and morality are transcended. Fourth, physical death is not the end of the Self; through the experience of cosmic consciousness, the fear of death is removed with the expectation that the *self* will reemerge in another form or dimension. Finally, in an impossibly complicated set of vague attitudinal predispositions, the nature of reality is regarded mystically through the altered consciousness of the individual which, in turn, construes or constructs reality to conform to a highly individualized and increasingly mystical definition (Sire, 2009, pp. 148-156). Thus the phrase popular today, "I am spiritual," usually reflects this perspective.

With these four Idea Systems in mind then, we can reconceptualize the cultural struggle taking place throughout the world as a series of **Worldviews in Conflict,** the very title of an excellent work by Christian historian Ronald H. Nash (1992) of the Reformed Theological Seminary in Orlando, Florida. Clearly, the Christian worldview is locked in mortal combat with the other three worldviews, the consequences of which will determine the direction of history itself in the foreseeable future. Here we are again reminded of Richard Weaver's seminal work, that indeed, Ideas Have Consequences (1948). And as I would often add in my graduate courses, "And Big Ideas have huge consequences."

FINAL NOTE ON THE STATE OF THE CHURCH

Before discussing the current spiritual health of the Christian church in America, some distinction needs to be made between it and Jewish Israel. It is the view of this writer that Christians and Jews have a distinctly different path to follow in the End Times. Briefly, we flatly reject the Replacement Theology view described earlier that eliminates the importance of Jews and the State of Israel, and regards the latter as having no place at all in eschatological discourse. Nothing could be further from doctrinal truth, since Jerusalem and Jewish Israel are both now and forever the very Center of the world and for that matter, the entire Universe.

This subject is too vast for extended discussion here, but for now we understand the literal prediction by the Apostle Paul that God has not "cast away His people" (Rom. 11:1, NKJV). On the epochal contrary, the prophet Zechariah explicitly predicts that Jerusalem will be one day surrounded by her enemies but will be delivered by God Himself, as "Jerusalem shall be raised up and inhabited in her place" and governed by the Lord in that Day (vv. 14:10, 16). In sum of a massive eschatological point: Jewish Israel is what Joel Rosenberg calls The Epicenter of all human history and political struggle, yesterday, again both today and forever (2006).

With that in mind then, there is grave cause for concern about the relative health of American Christianity today. Polls such as those published by Barna and others strongly warn of a church seriously misguided by contemporary trends, competing worldviews, and a growing indifference to the truth, especially among our younger people. Again, a clear index of Schaeffer's Accommodation thesis (1984). This in turn results in dramatic increase toward a state of being collectively *lukewarm*, as recorded by John's description of the Church of Laodicea (Rev. 3:14-22). Some clear evidence argues that the church is impacted more by the world than it is impacting the world.

Professor Gene Edward Veith, Jr. of Patrick Henry College, for example, pointed out years ago that 56 percent of single fundamentalist believers engage in sex outside of marriage, about the same rate as liberals (57 percent). According to the same report, 49 percent of Protestants and 47 percent of Catholics are "pro-choice" regarding abortion (Veith, 1994, p. 17). And we have heard numerous reports that Christians now divorce at a rate slightly exceeding the secular society, about 51 percent. Finally, a Pew Foundation poll recently found a concomitant and dramatic increase among Millennials becoming "Nones," or those eschewing any religious affiliation ("Nones on the Rise," 2012).

This is precisely why Jesus was so severe in His warnings to us about the Last Days in the Olivet Discourse. As we embark upon the beginning of those birth pangs leading up to the Great Tribulation and the terrifying Day of the Lord, we are currently in relatively poor condition for facing the tough times ahead. Indeed, the church appears to be abandoning a clearly articulated Judeo-Christian framework as it attempts to accommodate more and more Francis Schaeffer's "world spirit" idea (1984), rather than the other way around.

The Center of this battle that we now face, though played out in the cultural and ideological throes of battles over abortion, the immigration crisis, Islamic terrorism, an ostensible global warming, economic collapse and other woes, is inordinately about *Truth,* as mentioned in earlier sections of this work. Our best preparation for the times to come then is to be deeply embedded in God's Ideas in order to withstand the oceans of lies and deception and falsehood that already characterize our leading institutions in the media, our schools, government, and even the Church. We simply must wake up, before it is too late.

Chapter 4: The Second Seal Judgment

As we transition from the first to the second seal, notice as the white horse and rider go forth, there is a very real – though inherently deceptive – effort to make peace on the earth. As historian Paul Johnson (1983) makes eminently clear in his masterful treatment of world history from the 1920s through the 1980s, a preliminary effort at avoiding war through appeasement inevitably leads to the precipitation of war as we saw, again, in the Neville Chamberlain policies toward Hitler's Germany in pre-Second World War Europe. And, I quickly reiterate, in the ostensible peace negotiations with radically Islamic Iran to prevent them from securing nuclear capability. We will find here that this pattern is found once more, as the second seal is opened by the Lamb, for as quickly as the Antichrist proclaims a false "Peace and safety!" appeal, we see that a catastrophic series of wars break out upon the earth on the heels of that treacherous lie.

OPENING OF THE SECOND SEAL

And when He broke the second seal, I heard the second living creature saying, "Come." And another, a red horse, went out; and to him who sat on it, it was granted to take peace from the earth, and that men should slay one another; and a great sword was given to him. (Rev. 6:3-4)

In essence what we now have here is the first revelation of who the preceding rider of the first horse *truly* is. Once he has established himself firmly enough in the prevailing political order of the day, he launches his true intentions which are embodied in the resort to military combat. Scripture again warns severely the people of God concerning this eventuality: "Beware of the false prophets, who come to you in sheep's clothing, but inwardly are ravenous wolves. You will know them by their *fruits*" (Matt. 7:15-16; emph. added), the Greek term for fruits translating here as *results*. While at this point in history the Antichrist's true identity may not be widely known, those with discernment, wisdom and insight will begin to understand that he is not, in fact, who he claims to be (cf. Jn. 16:13; 2 Thess. 2:7). This will affix great responsibility upon believers to warn others of the impending conflicts still to come, as they see more and more of the reality of the age in which they are called to be a witness to the Truth.

In keeping with our parallelism between the Olivet Discourse and the Seal Judgments, we are reminded of Christ's words to the church in Matthew 24, verse 6: "And you will be hearing of wars and rumors of wars; see that you are not frightened, for those things must take place, but that is not yet the end" (cf. Mk. 13:7-8). Note the inescapable subtext here in which Christ clearly says that this is not yet "the end." Much more is yet to come, but these things are also regarded as mere birth pangs as I pointed out earlier. As I have repeatedly stated, neither, therefore, is this the Great Tribulation, but rather a combination of human and Satanic wrath being spread throughout the earth, again, with God's permission and even design, depending on your theology.

Rider on a Red Horse

Most commentators agree that the fiery red color of this horse strongly suggests bloodshed, and that symbolic bloodshed described in this passage is the direct result of *warfare and carnage* breaking out all over the earth. As with those birth pangs, these wars will begin to increase rapidly at some point in our not distant future. In fact, one could easily argue that this has already begun, as we witness the savagery that took place in Paris, France, and San Bernardino, California, recently. Then the 2016 Islamic assault on Brussels and later at Orlando, Florida as I write this paragraph. Thus one cannot underestimate the relevance here of this accelerating rise of Islam and ISIS as burgeoning agents of worldwide terror.

Note also, for example, in verse 4 that this rider is granted permission to "take peace from the earth." The Greek used here for the phrase "to take peace" is contextually defined as, *seize suddenly!* Clearly, it appears that many wars proliferate almost overnight at some point, as critical events escalate the conflicts at an increasingly heightened pace. Throughout the world, people and even little children begin to think and talk much of these wars and conflicts and widespread violence, which is the underlying explanation of why people begin to spread information about the wars, but also begin to speak frantically about "rumors of wars." As a consequence, gun stock and gun sales in the US are already skyrocketing as such rumors proliferate, alongside the former President's recent threat to increase his efforts at gun control (Aisch & Keller, 2016).

Men Should Slay One Another

Interesting that the translators should use the word "should" in relation to men slaying one another. Without reading too much into the text, this is suggestive of a New Normal in the earth. That is, the old order of "Peace and safety!" is clearly replaced with a new expectation. Indeed, that it somehow is now expected or even right to slay one another on the field of battle, though I quickly add that I don't believe that the "field of battle" is the only arena for such slaughter. It is quite probable that the entire earth and her many cities, are themselves become bloody battlefields with the associate expectation of increasing levels of what is called "collateral damage" – i.e., the killing of innocent civilians. This with increased terrorism in our cities, gang related violence and other crimes of assault soaring, we are already witnessing this increased mayhem in city after city both here and abroad.

The word for "slay" in this passage, for example, is found in the Greek term, *sphazo,* coming from a root word meaning, "to butcher or maim or wound severely." Thus is described a savage time when men and women and even small children are literally slaughtering each other on battlefields and in cities throughout the world. Sound familiar? As savage example, even the New York Times recently noted the virtual genocide of Christians in the Middle East by ISIS and its Muslim Jihadist counterparts, as journalist Eliza Griswold fairly shouted in the title of her powerful essay: "Is This the End of Christianity in the Middle East?" (2015).

Thus as the fog of war descends upon the planet more and more thickly, a spiritual landscape of physical darkness begins to pervade the nations. Theologian John Walvoord describes these dark times in unmistakable terms:

> [T]he constant tension among nations and the ambitions of men have their climax in this period before Christ comes. Though 'wars and rumors of wars' ... are characteristic of the Age, it is evident that warfare occupies a large place in the consummation of the age with resultant great loss of life. There apparently is a series of wars, the greatest of which is under way at the time of the second coming. (as cited in Gregg, 1997, p. 107)

Thus what we see here according to this view are a number of limited conflicts inevitably escalating over a period of several years as run up to the final and catastrophic Battle of Armageddon at the very end of the time of Great Tribulation.

A Great Sword

The meaning of "a great sword" also helps us to understand the barbarism of this time on the earth. One rendering of this sword points out that it "is not the large two-edged sword (see v. 8) but the dagger used in hand-to-hand combat" (Easley & Anders, 1999, p. 107). The implication here is that not only are there fully weaponized armies going to war, but also individuals or ordinary citizens who possess small arms fire for use against one another. Thus do we see, as mentioned in the NY Times piece earlier, Americans rushing to purchase firearms as never before for personal protection. In the spirit of full disclosure, I am unapologetically one of those Americans.

Still another interpretation – my own this time – is brought to us by the words used to describe a "great" sword in verse 4. The Greek term here is *megas,* which refers quite literally to that which is "huge" or "loud," causing massive noise and widespread loss of life and fearsome consequences. I cannot help but conceive of the somewhat limited use of weapons of mass destruction at this point in history, or those WMDs we hear and read so much about in the form of nuclear, biological and chemical means of dispatching large numbers of people in a single day. One chilling example of this would be where the Jihadists targeted a nuclear plant in their prelude to constructing a Radiological Dispersal Device (RDD, or "dirty bomb") to contaminate a large regional area and create widespread panic. This of course would be a political and military game changer (Moran, 2015).

Henry Morris points out a fact that is so obvious as to be overwhelming when we consider all of world history. As I perused the Internet while preparing this section, I looked up the term "war" and found no fewer than 397,000,000 hits. As I looked at various summaries of world history in particular, I discovered what we ought to already know: Mankind's entire existence is synonymous with warfare. As Morris observes: "It is an amazing thing that men, created in the image of God, should become so blinded with hate or lust or ambition or envy that they should seek to destroy the precious lives of others. Yet the very first man born in the world slew his brother, and men have followed in the way of Cain ever since" (1983, p. 113). Both Morris and Gregg also see this time of warfare involving many civil wars, organized crime wars, and individual feuds generating "waves of murders" (see Gregg, 1997, p. 109). Again I add, sadly, that there is even growing evidence of race wars heating up in the United States (Starkes, 2013).

Thus that "great sword" is great indeed, inclusive of all categories of mayhem and slaughter imaginable throughout the whole earth and all its cities and villages. It will, in effect, be a time of widespread violence everywhere, with people feeling unsafe to go out for fear of being harmed or killed or captured and tortured. The great Culture War in America to which I often refer may quickly devolve into a Civil War if left unchecked by reason and morality and sound, strong and principled political leadership.

More painfully to us as parents here at home, still more slaughters like those at Columbine High in Littleton, Colorado in 1999, Virginia Tech in 2007, Sandy Hook Elementary School in 2012, and Umpqua Community College in Oregon in 2015 could occur as our young people become increasingly disillusioned with the current wave of hypocritical and grossly compromised leadership of our elder statesmen. And we have hardly mentioned the news and entertainment media that fuels and feeds a culture of violence wherever there is a television set to receive grotesque images of murder and violence (cf. Gerbner & Gross, 1976; Postman, 1985).

Alluding again to our parallel to Christ's Olivet Discourse, Matthew 24:12 describes this seal clearly: "And because *lawlessness is increased,* most people's love will grow cold" (emph. added). The presence of worldwide conflict and outright warfare is accompanied by the absence of a socio-political peace, which may be regarded synonymously with the presence of *chaos.* Another interesting term, "chaos" is defined by a Hebrew term in Isaiah 24:10 as *tohu,* or "formlessness, confusion, unreality, emptiness, desolation, waste place," and a sense of massive disorder. In sum, a spirit of lawlessness (or forms of Anarchism and/or Antinomianism) pervades the nations more and more as the chaos spreads.

This is precisely where the term, "the fog of war," originates. War is the presence of overwhelming uncertainty and fear, as events careen from destruction to destruction in the effort for one side to defeat the other. We saw this phenomenon years ago in the unprecedented, horrific attack on the twin towers in New York City on September 11, 2001, savagery on a whole new scale by Islamic terrorists on American soil. This event is indeed regarded by many as the formal beginning of World War III, since its occurrence ramifies throughout most of the entire world. But an even earlier date serves as a harbinger of things yet to come upon the United States and the world, as Islam reinstitutes its efforts to conquer and control the entire planet.

THE THREAT OF ISLAMIC TERRORISM

On June 5, 1968, Sirhan Bishara Sirhan fired a .22 caliber pistol at the head of Robert F. Kennedy at the Ambassador Hotel in Los Angeles, California, fatally wounding the presumptive next President of the United States. Sirhan's stated motive was Kennedy's support of Israel in the 1967 Six Day War. Born into a Palestinian Christian family who later become a Rosicrucian (cf. Pagan Mysticism), Sirhan's violent act at the very least signaled a resumption or new beginning of Middle East-based terrorism aimed against America and the Western world. That one act highlighted an underlying rage that exists on the part of many Palestinians (who are mostly Muslim), who for a variety of reasons despise all of Western Judeo-Christianity, the members of which are viewed as threats to Middle Eastern autonomy. In effect, it may well have served as the fuse that lit the nascent origins of that Third World War between East and West (see Huntington, 1996).

We indeed see evidence of such a war in the fiery rubble of September 11, 2001 in New York City and Washington, DC, and in the "Islamic" murder of RFK. The importance of these two events separated by 33 years cannot be overstated. I am convinced that the world is now engaged in an historic, titanic struggle which will, ultimately, largely define the course of human history. Indeed, this battle or more appropriately, this

58

World War in which we are now inextricably involved, is by many accounts a struggle for civilization itself (see Carl F.H. Henry, Twilight of a Great Civilization, 1988). In the words of still another Christian theologian, Ravi Zacharias, we must understand that this massive struggle between Eastern Islam and Western Judeo-Christianity is a "revolution ... plagued with what we now call 'the mystery of wickedness,'" or what others label again as the *mysterium tremendum* – a description of activities so vile that they defy human understanding (see Zacharias, 1996, p. xv).

The roots of this revolution leading to World War are to be found in the vastly conflicting ideas or ideologies or what I term "civilizational worldviews" which collide in increasingly violent and unrelenting protest of the other's existence. Not unlike nor since Robert George's Clash of Orthodoxies (2001), have we witnessed so pervasive a spread of warlike tendencies throughout the earth based on radically different religious and political ideologies. The key point here is that there is an inexorable *linkage* between one's religious worldview and one's overt actions, a point made crystal clear in Dr. David Noebel's Understanding the Times, where he flatly proposed that "Every individual bases his thoughts and actions on a worldview" (1994, p. 1). As Proverbs 23:7a affirms, "For as a man thinks, so he is." To understand the present war over religious ideas, we must fully appreciate and understand this linkage.

Terrorism, then, is a term that could well describe the *zeitgeist* or characterizing framework which governs our world today. Shafritz offers a definition of *terrorism* that helps us to understand the far-reaching implications of this second seal judgment: "Highly visible violence directed against randomly selected civilians in an effort to generate a pervasive sense of fear and thus affect government policies" (1988, p. 542). So this is the nature of the New War of today's world, an unconventional guerilla-type assault on Western peoples and institutions designed to completely destroy them through the use of almost randomly selected, largely civilian targets by any means necessary.

Origins of Islam: The "Prophet" Muhammed

This approach to fomenting a worldwide clash of civilizations largely finds its origins, of course, in the founder of Islam, the so-called "prophet" of Islam, or Islamism, Muḥammad (or Mohammed) ibnʿAbdullāh, or more plainly, Muhammed (570-632 A.D.). Countless biographies have been published about this mysterious figure. While there is not enough space here to detail that biography, it must be shown that today's militant Islam would not have been possible without Mohammed's personal migration from his earlier, milder form of Islam to the more violent forms exhibited by his followers we see so often today.

The historical records demonstrate that following his "revelations" from an ostensible angel named Gabriel, this then-new religious system culminated in the written book, the Qur'an. Based on this authoritative text gradually compiled over a period of approximately 23 years, beginning on 22 December 609 AD, when Mohammad was 40, and concluding in 632, the year of his death, Muhammed began his efforts to convert the then Jewish or pagan people of the area by peaceful means.

However, and this is an epic "however," seeing that such methods were ineffective, he turned to more successful military means, significantly, aiming more and more *against the Jews* who inhabited the region:

> Mohammed then turned his attention once again to the Jews, who were easier targets then the Meccans. He began killing the Jews and looting Jewish settlements. After one Jewish town had surrendered, 700 to 1,000 men were beheaded in one day while all the women and children were sold into slavery and the possessions of the town looted! This fact is supported by Muslim

scholars as well as by Western historians. (Morey, 1992, p. 83; cf. Dashti, 1985, pp. 89-91)

Thus are the roots of militant Islam found entrenched in the earliest chronicles of Muslim conquests and barbarism toward anyone who would not peaceably convert.

Therefore, Islam came to mean something that is predicated on the impenetrable, unquestioned dogma of the Qur'an (see Gibb & Kramers, 1953, p. 276). The definition of "Islam" in turn is noted by Dr. Mark Hartwig: "Islam in its original meaning is the primary act of self-surrender: an act of ... choice whereby a person places his or her destiny in the hands of Allah and *submits* to Allah's government" (2002b, p. 18; emph. added). The implications of this relatively moderate statement are found squarely in the center of the word, **submit.**

Clear to us today is the reality that Islam is devoted to a worldwide effort to establish an Islamic Caliphate in every country on earth, and thus must its orthodox adherents be so as well. The scope of this vision is nothing short of earthshaking, and more will be said of this a bit later.

The Concept of Jihad

Thus also was found the birth of something called *Jihad,* regarded by some as the Sixth Pillar of Islam (the first five being comprised of the reciting of the Shahadah, Prayer, Almsgiving, Fasting, and Pilgrimage to Mecca). Dr. Mark Hartwig again defines Jihad: "Although the term jihad means 'struggle' rather than 'war,' physical combat is clearly part of the concept ... The Holy Qur'an [which means "recitation"] has given a comprehensive treatment to its concept of war. The book defines and determines all aspects of the use of 'force' in interstate relations ... and prescribes its own rules and principles for the conduct of war" (2002a, p. 4). So the question now becomes, what are those rules or teachings concerning the conduct of war?

We turn, therefore to the first of **three sources** of information about those rules of engagement, the Qur'an. These Quranic verses, or "surahs" are taken from a translation by A. Y. Ali, The Meaning of the Holy Quran (2001). An early entry reflects that more peaceful approach taken by Mohammed as he began his ministry. "Invite (all) to the way of the Lord with wisdom and beautiful preaching; and argue with them in ways that are best and most gracious; for the Lord knoweth best, who have strayed from His path, and who receive guidance" (16:125).

Later, however, we see that *marked shift* in the rhetoric of the Qur'an as demonstration of the Islamic Principle of Abrogation, and its tactics of warfare. "But when the forbidden months are past, then fight and slay the pagans [non-Muslims] wherever ye find them, and seize them, beleaguer them, and lie in wait for them in every stratagem (of war); but if they repent, and establish regular prayers and practice regular charity, then open the way for them; for God is oft-forgiving, Most Merciful" (9:5).

Even more to the point of this analysis, the Qur'an makes very clear who its main enemies are in the following passage, again, from the warlike 9th Sura. "Fight those who believe not in God nor the Last Day, nor hold forbidden which hath been forbidden by God and His Apostle, nor acknowledge the religion of Truth, (even if they are) of the People of the Book [Christians and Jews], until they pay the jizya [tribute] with willing submission, and feel themselves *subdued*" (9:29; cf. Hartwig, 2002b, p. 27; emph. added). One cannot, again, escape the notion of absolute submission implied in the word, "subdued." This is a religious system that will, in sum, use any and all means to conquer the infidels – which refers of course to all non-Muslims – but especially to "People of The Book," or Bible honoring Jews and Christians.

A second source of information describing the Islamic approach to militant evangelization and conquest is found in the Hadith. This is a collection of Muslim traditions which, according to Morey, "record the words and deeds of Muhammed according to his wives, family members, friends and Muslim leaders which are not usually found in the Quran" (Morey, 1992, p. 177). The quotations which follow are taken from the translation by M. M. Khan, The Translation of the Meaning of Sahih Al-Bukhari (1997). Let's take a brief look at these "sayings" concerning warfare:

- *On Jihad.* "Allah's Apostle was asked, 'What is the best deed?' He replied, 'To believe in Allah and his Apostle [Muhammed].' The questioner then asked, 'What is the next [in goodness]?' He replied: 'To participate in Jihad [religious fighting] in Allah's cause" (vol. 1, no. 25).
- *On Jihad.* "People are to be either converted or subdued through violence of military force" (vol. 1, p. xxii).
- *On Killing.* "The Prophet said, 'Whoever has killed an enemy and has proof of that, will possess his spoils" (vol. 1, no. 24).
- *On Killing.* "No Muslim should be killed for killing an infidel" (vol. 4, no. 283; vol. 9, no. 50).
- *On Heaven.* "Any Muslim who is killed while fighting in a Jihad will go straight to the sexual pleasures of Paradise" (vol. 1, no. 35; vol. 4, no. 386).
- *On Apostasy.* "The Prophet said, 'If somebody [a Muslim] discard his religion [of Islam], kill him" (vol. 4, no. 260).
- *On People of the Book.* "Any Jews or Christians who heard about me and did not believe in me and what was revealed to me of the Holy Quran and my traditions, his ultimate destination is the [Hell] fire" (vol. 1, p. li).

Thus we clearly see the war-mongering policies and principles of the Qur'an affirmed, elaborated and deepened by the sayings of the sacred Hadith.

Our final source of information about how to conduct war according to Islam is found in the mouths of *the terrorists* themselves. A few of them are quoted here, largely taken from Steven Emerson's revealing book, American Jihad (2002), published within one year of the devastations of 9/11:

- *Emerson's Testimony.* "Once I found myself at a Muslim convention where a speaker started shouting, 'Steven Emerson is the enemy of Islam! Are we going to let him tell us what to do?' 'No,' the crowd roared in response ... then the death threats began" (pp. 14-15).

- *On Towers.* "In a small wire-bound notebook, [El-Sayeed] Nosair [the murderer of Rabbi Meir Kahane] had written, 'We have to thoroughly demoralize the enemies of God by means of destroying and blowing up the towers that constitute the pillars of their civilization such as the tourist attractions they are so proud of and the high buildings they are so proud of'" (p. 44; Nov. 5, 1990, nearly 11 years before they brought down the Twin Towers in New York City).

- *On a War with America.* "I don't think there's a war here, a war front here in the United States at this point [1994]. I think if the whole scenario continues the way it has, inevitably the United States is going to be reaching a type of war front. Yeah. But not right now" (p. 61; Mohammed Al-Asi, of the Islamic Center in Potomac, Maryland, from a television documentary, Jihad in America).

- *On Suicide.* "I say, it is not correct when some people say that we commit suicide because we do not value life. We love life, but life in dignity ... I cannot allow God's houses to be violated without defending them ... At the Law Faculty of Al-Azhar University I was about to receive a certificate in law, but in this phase I prefer another kind of certificate, the other life, *martyrdom in the path of God*...Finally I pray to Almighty God that my action may result in the death of the greatest number of God's enemies as possible" (p. 101; Hamdi Yasin, who died while killing an Israeli officer by driving his car into a military checkpoint).

The Ultimate Terror

Thus far we have presupposed that Islamic warfare against the West will be and has been largely conventional. That is, through the use of weapons such as bombs, missiles, rifles, knives, mortars, rocket propelled grenades and the like. But there is another level of terror, one so unspeakable and suggested by the last quotation above from the late Hamdi Yasin, that it qualifies as belonging in the family of that *mysterium tremendum* noted earlier. We conclude this chapter on warfare, then, with an introduction of the ultimate terror that Islamic militants are planning to use as a next step in the war against the West.

During the month of May 2003, Nasser bin Hamad Al-Fahd issued what would become the marching orders for the next generation of Islamic terrorists. Its title: "The Nuclear Fatwa … A Treatise on the Legal Status of Using Weapons of Mass Destruction Against Infidels." Reprinted in full in Paul Williams' The Day of Islam (2007), it carves out a chilling set of arguments with such subtitles as "The Basic Rule in Killing Is to Do It in a Good Manner," "Distinguishing between the Possible and the Impossible," "The Permissibility of Attacking the Polytheists by Night, Even if Their Children Are Injured," "The Permissibility of Burning the Enemy's Lands," and finally, "The Permissibility of Striking the Enemy with Weapons That Cause Mass Destruction" (pp. 213-223).

Al Queda commander Rakan ben Williams in March 2006 stated the objectives of this next phase of war with the West:

> Let me inform you about your inability to stop them [nuclear attacks on US soil] before they are carried out. The reason is simple; you cannot uncover or stop them except by letting them be carried out. Furthermore, the best you could do would be to accelerate the day of

carrying out the operations. In other words, if we schedule the operation to take place tomorrow, the best you could do is to make it happen today ... I will not give any more clues; this is enough as a wake-up call. Perhaps the American people will start thinking about the magnitude of the danger that is coming their way. (as cited in Williams, 2007, pp. 207-208)

All of which stands in stunning contrast to the West's principles of waging what most nations in the Christian West call a *Just War* (see Charles, 2005). In that historic set of guidelines are included, for example, such issues as a Just Cause, Proper Authority, Right Intention, Discrimination, and Proportionality. Of particular concern is the protection of innocent civilians (see Ch. 7). The staggering question that emerges here is this: Can a Just War be effectively waged with a completely lawless, barbarous foe? Ponder this very carefully. Our generals and admirals certainly are.

Finally, the most savage and recent iteration of Jihadism has come to us in the form of ISIS – the Islamic State of Iraq and Syria. In his personally compelling, exhaustively researched and thoroughly biblical analysis of that group and its rapid conquests, former Liberty University vice president and current CEO of a public relations agency and more importantly, world humanitarian, Johnnie Moore bluntly and accurately observes that "The goal of ISIS from the very beginning has been to ethnically cleanse their land, and eventually the world, of Christians," and, I must add, Jews (2015, p. 9). This worldwide terrorist wave continues to carry out its mission to thus far, a completely and somewhat inexplicably ineffectual American response.

Yet this is mere surface scratch compared to the deep structure analysis of the very roots of Mohammed's theology, Sharia Law, and the historic Islamic mandate for worldwide Jihad by the now outlawed (by the Obama administration) expert on Muslim hegemony, Stephen Coughlin. In his massive contribution to our understanding of Islamic thought in Catastrophic Failure: Blindfolding America in the Face of Jihad (2015), he outlines the contours of the nation's fate if we continue to ignore the core tenets of Muslim faith to conquer the West by what we here consider to be nothing less than savagery to destroy us, and Israel. He is a must read for further insight into America's colossal ignorance of the true threat of Islam to our very survival. In sum: Our very existence as a free republic depends on our understanding and opposing militant Islam with every resource at our Constitutional disposal.

In all of this we are left with a presently crippling moral and tactical dilemma. As today's wars and skirmishes come to us increasingly and more and more intensely, how is it that we are to fight back based on Judeo-Christian Just War principles when the other side will not fight accordingly? The implications for American and Israeli foreign policies are far reaching indeed, and enormously complex. We are up against a foe the likes of which we have never seen before, even during World War II. Clearly, we will need the brightest and bravest minds available in the days just ahead, along with God's unmistakable hand of guidance. But the current political scene does not auger well for such wisdom, to state it in the kindest of terms.

FINAL NOTES ON WORLD CONFLICT

Throughout the last 30 years or so, as I drilled down on these weighty matters, it became more and more apparent that the locus of virtually all human conflict is that of Israel, or more specifically, *Jerusalem*. There is ample biblical and historical evidence for such a view. The Scriptures tell us of this, for example, in no uncertain terms: "And it will come about in that day that I will make Jerusalem a heavy stone for all the peoples; all who lift it will be severely injured. And all the nations of the earth will be gathered against it." (Zech. 12:3)

Indeed, Islam's most furious attentions are focused on Israel, and more particularly upon Jerusalem.

More pointedly then, both past and current peace talks between representatives of the United States, Israel and the various Islamic entities continue to debate over who shall own and control this great city – Jews or Muslims. This conflict has become especially intense since the Israelis took back the city in the Six Day War of 1967, and remains a current topic of debate at this writing after then President Barack Obama struck his recent, controversial "Deal" with Iran (see Hanson, 2015).

Another central focus of bloody conflict in the world has to do with a practice that tragically remains off the political radar in America and other nations: *Abortion.* Referred to by some as a Second Holocaust, I view the second seal judgment as also inclusive of the presence of the massive bloodshed of the pre-born throughout the earth. Clearly, the roughly 60 million dead children in the U.S. alone since *Roe v. Wade* was established by the Supreme Court in 1973 qualify as such a holocaust of even biblical proportion. Carnage of this kind is unprecedented in the world, and as David Wilkerson warned some years ago, "We can be assured that not a single baby's slaughter will go unnoticed by our God of justice. He promises to ... [make] inquisition for blood ... He remembereth them: He forgetteth not the cry of the humble" (cf. Psalm 9:12; Wilkerson, 1998, pp. 45-46). Recent grisly accounts of Planned Parenthood's harvesting dead baby body parts for profit beggar human understanding, and widespread media indifference to its indisputable video exposure by the Center for Medical Progress (Houck, 2015).

This warning was surrounded in Wilkerson's estimation by another issue of critical importance to students and scholars of the Last Days: a coming economic crisis, the subject of our next chapter.

Chapter 5: The Third Seal Judgment

Most Americans today are feeling the intensity of a financial crisis building largely on the heels, arguably of course, of the declining American dollar, Chinese stock market declines and market manipulations, and the European financial chaos like that which we saw in Greece in recent years. Even as I write these words, the Dow Jones Industrial Average was in near freefall, but later steadier (Young, 2016). In fact, on June 24, 2016, the markets plunged wildly on the heels of the Brexit vote in the UK to withdraw from the European Union. This a serious, possibly temporary blow, to the Globalist vision described in Daniel 7:23 as precursor to "the fourth beast" (or kingdom) that shall rule with an iron fist as a worldwide union in the Last Days. So while these present economic challenges are vastly more complex than this simple analysis proposes, most experts agree that America, the West and entire world are headed for, and are already firmly within, stormy economic times.

Founder of the highly regarded journal, American Thinker, and former Harvard business professor Thomas Lifson, for example, issued this dark warning in a recent issue: "The world will be unable to fight the next global financial crash as central banks have used up their ammunition trying to tackle the last crises, the Bank of International Settlements has warned" (2015, para. 3). Thus it is in the third seal judgment that we see the true nature and impact of this looming financial crisis.

THE OPENING OF THE THIRD SEAL

And when He broke the third seal, I heard the third living creature saying, "Come" And I looked, and behold, a black horse; and he who sat on it had a pair of scales in his hand. And I heard as it were a voice in the center of the four living creatures saying, "A quart of wheat for

*a denarius, and three quarts of barley for a denarius;
and do not harm the oil and the wine."* (Rev. 6:5-6)

So here we see still another horse and rider, who follow the other two which symbolized: (1) the white horse and rider who ride forth in order to "conquer" but not yet by warfare, but by false promises of peace and safety; then (2) the red horse and rider who go forth to take that false peace from the earth, and thus bring about worldwide war and bloodshed. We can see still again that the one begets the other – i.e., a deceptive peace engenders a very real and physical war as the populace discovers the truth of those geopolitical sleights of hand. And these in their combined turns yield an increasingly unstable world economy. I might also remind here that if the rider on the first horse is the Antichrist as most commentaries propose, then it is axiomatic that warfare, massive instability, and chaos was what he had in mind all along.

A Black Horse

The Greek word for "black" is *melas,* meaning quite literally, "as black as ink." The resident contextual implication is that black represents a time of great *mourning,* as the trials and difficulties in the world grow still more intense. It is indeed a very dark time that this seal describes, a consequence of the increasing intensity of the times. One can envision masses of people – men, women and especially little children – weeping under the pressures brought by this seal.

Most commentaries again regard this color as indicative also of the conditions under which people experience increased absence of the basic necessities of food and water, which also of course add to the general spirit of mourning and worry that spreads throughout the earth as people wonder how to pay the bills. In point of fact, Matthew 24:7 predicts that there will be increased conflicts among nations and people groups, along with "famines and earthquakes." Of all these events, the idea of *famine* is preeminent here, a concept we will develop as we move into this chapter's discussion more deeply.

A Pair of Scales

Depending on whose commentary you consult, these scales indicate the possible presence of (a) "scarcity" (Ladd, 1972, p. 100); (b) "famine" (Hendley, 1985, p. 85); then (c) "starving" (Stewart, 2008, p. 3); and (d) "hunger" and "prices extremely high" (Stewart, 2008, p. 3). Putting this together in a single profile strongly suggests a time in the world when the prices of goods and commodities will soar, with the concomitant presence of increasing levels of food and commodity scarcity – which in turn drives up the prices of those goods and services. Precisely what the world is increasingly experiencing today. We see the cost of virtually everything going up precipitously, with as much as 17% to 75% increases on most commodities based on six major factors (cf. Troutman, 2015). At the same time, stock market rises and subsequent declines continue since their peak in October 2014, as a quick look at your smart phone stocks app graph will amply demonstrate.

Thus in verse 6 of Revelation 6, we find more of the answer to the question raised about harsh economic times. It states, "a quart of wheat" and "three quarts of barley" will cost "a denarius." Historians tell us that a denarius in Christ's day was essentially the amount of money a man would need for his daily sustenance, or what the common laborer would earn in a day. As a result we see a severe economic condition in which a man or woman would have to work an entire day just to feed themselves for that day. To feed an entire family would become more and more unachievable, forcing some to take up criminal acts or begging on the streets in order to provide for the household.

What all of this would likely mean to the nation and world is a return to a time of food and gasoline rationing, as we experienced during the Second World War. Thus the penetrating message here describes not only a time of paucity of necessary goods and services, but also hyperinflation, increased unemployment and applications for welfare – facts already dramatically evident in today's economy (cf. Worstall, 2015). In sum, a world drawn more and more into a degree of financial chaos that it had never before experienced.

Webster's classic 1828 Dictionary of the English Language defines "famine" as "scarcity of food; dearth ... [related to] famish ... to be exhausted in strength, or to come near to perish, for want of food or drink." While these circumstances are not presently occurring on a wide scale in the United States, there will come a time – perhaps in the not too distant future if trends continue – in which these things will be the reality. At the beginning of those birth pangs we will likely see the early seeds of this condition, as with the rises in the cost of fuels and food stuffs. The trend line is suggestive of a deepening and worsening of these circumstances. While I used to pray that such things do not occur in our lifetimes, I am become strongly convinced that we must *be prepared* as they appear to be coming true in just the next few years. More on this in the Epilogue.

One summary view of the economic times in which we live describes the overall nature and source of our current trouble as we look back to a pivotal economic year for America.

> The United States, the world's largest economy, entered 2008 during a housing market correction, a subprime mortgage crisis and a declining dollar value. In February, 63,000 jobs were lost, a five-year record. On July 11, the largest mortgage lender in the US collapsed. IndyMac Bank's assets were seized by federal regulators after the mortgage lender succumbed to the pressures of tighter credit, tumbling home prices and rising foreclosures. That day the financial markets plunged as investors tried to gauge whether the government would

attempt to save mortgage lenders (Gwartney, 2009, p. 2).

The article went on to cite numerous statistics which clearly showed an unprecedented, worldwide economic crisis in such places as Europe, New Zealand, South Africa and Asia which collectively ramped up global inflation. The analysis suggested that the entire world was increasingly in the grip of unsolvable economic woes that would ultimately touch most of the planet's population. And today's world inflation rate is predicted to be no less than 3.5% by the International Monetary Fund, with other sources projecting even higher rates. ("Slower Growth," 2015)

Fast forward to 2016, when the Dow was in still another phase of radical fluctuations, and we cannot deny that very clearly, something both national and global is afoot. It is possible that by the time these words are fit to publish early in 2017, things will have improved. Or not.

The Power of Famine

Most Americans find it inconceivable that we would ever get to the point of the nationwide famine alluded to earlier. Most of us are well fed from stores brimming with the necessary foodstuffs that we all depend on for our health and well-being. But the Bible unequivocally portends a time when the world economy will be such that a literal famine will gradually envelop the earth. I recall reading Billy Graham's classic publication many years ago, Approaching Hoofbeats: The Four Horsemen of the Apocalypse (1984), which warned of these events long before the present crises emerged:

> Since the beginning of time there has been famine on the face of the earth. But with the population explosion and the complexity of modern society, the problem of the hungry has greatly increased. No one knows how many die of starvation each year ... [but] The Mennonite Central Committee reports that an estimated 12 million

newborn infants die of the effects of malnutrition every year in the developing countries. The World Bank reports that "half of the people in absolute poverty live in South Asia, mainly in India and Bangladesh. A sixth live in East and Southeast Asia. Another sixth are in sub-Saharan Africa. The rest are divided among Latin America, North Africa and the Middle East." The United Nations estimates that at least 100 million children go to bed each night hungry. But the problem of hunger and malnutrition is not limited to developing countries. Recently the Congressional Office of the Budget announced that many of America's children, too, suffer greatly from malnutrition. (pp. 154-155)

An even more recent summary of the presence of famine in the world observed that over 795 million people are in a condition of critical hunger ("2015 World Hunger," 2015). In America alone these days, over 49 million people suffer already from hunger, and our poverty rate has increased dramatically since 2008, according to most studies ("Hunger & Poverty Factsheet," 2015). If the Bible is true, then we can expect this terrible plague to visit America, as well, in the years to come.

The true power of famine, however, is captured not only in groups of faceless statistics but by the Scriptures themselves. In a truly stunning passage from the Old Testament, famine's viciousness is described in detail:

Now it came about after this, that Ben-hadad king of Aram gathered all his army and went up and besieged Samaria. And there was a great famine in Samaria; and behold, they besieged it, until a donkey's head was sold for eighty shekels of silver, and a fourth of a kab [or 2 quarts] of dove's dung for five shekels of silver. And as the king of Israel was passing by on the wall a woman cried out to him, saying, "Help, my lord, O king!" And he said, "If the Lord does not help you, from where shall I help you? From the threshing floor, or from the wine press?" And the king said to her, "What is the matter with you?" And she answered, "This woman said to me, 'Give me your son that we may eat him today, and we will eat my son tomorrow.'" So we boiled my son and ate him; and I said to her on the next day, "Give your son, that we may eat him"; but she has hidden her son. (2 Kings 6:24-29)

Inconceivable. Impossible. Inhuman. Abominable. Bestial. Yet such is the raw power of unsatisfied hunger taken to the extremes of the scarcity of food to eat.

As pointed out earlier, it is significant that the presence of war in the second seal works in devastating harmony with the famine of the third seal. As the earth continues to reap the harvest of dramatic political realignments such as those taking place today, worldwide wars and now hunger and famine, we see that *war helps to fuel famine* by: (1) destroying the fields used for planting; (2) as men are drafted and conscripted into military service, the supply of farmers is diminished; and (3) the few farmers remaining are discouraged because what they do plant will be plundered by invading troops.

And of course, God forbid, there is an ominous fourth reason: If there is any nuclear exchange, the lands involved are rendered useless for hundreds, even thousands, of years. Thus Iran's threats to annihilate Israel and even America with either a nuclear attack or other weapons of mass destruction no more become the rantings of a crazed terrorist nation, but a possible, if presently remote, reality in today's increasingly violent and chaotic world.

Another observation regarding the impact of a worldwide economic and hunger crisis needs to be noted. In a report by USA Today a few years ago, journalist Marilyn Elias states mental health experts were seeing dramatic increases in Americans seeking treatment for such ills as anxiety, depression, sleep problems and money-rooted marital conflicts. More specifically, she reported that requests for therapists increased "15% to 20% in the past three months, primarily driven by concerns about the financial situation," according to Richard Chaifetz, neuropsychologist and chairman and CEO of ComPsych in Chicago, the nation's largest employee-assistance mental health program with more than 24 million members (as cited in Elias, 2008, p. 1A). Most of us can closely relate to the severe pain and pressures involved in not having enough money to cover the bills and buy enough food to feed our families. We are already experiencing these pressures in 21st century America, as one report shows 51 percent of Americans today living on an annual income of less than $30,000 (Snyder, 2015).

Final mention should also be made about the very real and growing threat by our adversaries to shut down America's power grid. More specifically, much has recently been written and spoken about regarding the increasing possibility of an EMP (Electromagnetic Pulse) attack through the detonation of a nuclear weapon several hundred miles above the center of the nation. Norman Rogers, writing for American Thinker, wrote an excellent piece about what this would do:

> A single nuclear bomb, exploded 400 miles above Kansas, could wipe out much of the electronic and electrical infrastructure of the USA. Automobiles, trucks, and railroad engines might be so electronically damaged as to no longer operate. In any case, fuel would be difficult to obtain due to lack of electricity and due to destruction of the electronic control (SCADA systems) of refineries and pipelines. Electricity could be absent for months or years. The novel One Second After is a fictional account of what happens in a small town when an EMP strikes. (2015, para. 18)

Thus with the country plunged into nearly total darkness, with no power to access the basic necessities of life (food, water, heat, travel, etc.), the effects of the Third Seal would be magnified once again to, quite literally, biblical proportion. Famine writ massive in scope would prevail all the more, and the loss of life would obviously become almost unimaginable.

As a rather intriguing side note, journalist Ted Koppel's compelling recent book, Lights Out (2015), describes the devastating consequences of such a cyberattack, pointing out that there are three major grids in America. One is called the East Coast Grid, the second is the West Coast Grid, and the third: Texas. It is no secret to anyone these days that love or hate it, Texas is pretty much the Last Bastion of a traditionally realistic Christian conservativism, its pockets of more liberal communities notwithstanding.

The Oil and the Wine

More happily however, in an intriguing conclusion to the Third Seal, the voice of the four living creatures warns, "and do not harm the oil and the wine" (Rev. 6:6). Many commentators and theologians have puzzled over this mysterious phrase for decades. Charles Ryrie, for example, wrote: "Apparently luxury items will not be in short supply, but of course most people will not be able to afford them. This situation will only serve to taunt the populace in their impoverished state" (as cited in Gregg, 1997, p. 113). Or as Ironside wrote, "The rich seem to escape a part of this judgment for the oil and the wine, the luxuries of the well to do, are not to be hurt … They will receive their share of judgment later, however" (as cited in Gregg, 1997, p. 113).

While these interpretations are plausible, I don't believe that they strike the intended or contextual mark. As I have argued throughout, Christians will still be here as these judgments are meted out since they do not represent the true Wrath of God, but are rather more indicative of Satan's wrath.

Further, the concepts of the oil and the wine are here taken to be more symbolic than literal if I am correct. And they most closely associate, on that allegorical level, with *believers* who are described in veiled terms like the "oil" (the Holy Spirit within us) and the "wine" (the Blood of Christ by which we are purchased).

More specifically, if the Rapture has indeed not yet occurred as I believe, then there is here a magnificent proclamation of *some* degree of **divine protection** for all true followers of the True Messiah. While the impact of these critical economic times will in some way touch most people of the earth, the obedient body of Christ is at least partially protected from their effects. That is, there is a degree of special "covering" for Christians implied in this passage that lends great hope to those of us alive at this time, as war, economic chaos, hunger, famine and other ills pervade the earth more and more. In such a scenario, we become places of refuge for those seeking shelter from the economic and associate storms.

In some support of these ideas, the prophet Jeremiah eloquently promises such measured protection and provision in times of trial and distress. "Blessed is the man who trusts in the Lord and whose trust is the Lord. For he will be like a tree planted by the water, that extends its roots by a stream and will not fear when the heat comes; But its leaves will be green, and it will not be anxious in a year of drought nor cease to yield fruit" (Jer. 17:7-8).

In still another passage, this time from the prophet Isaiah, it is likewise promised that in a time of great distress we will be treated differently by God than those who have no relationship to Him. "Arise, shine; for your light has come, and the glory of the Lord has risen upon you. For behold, darkness will cover the earth and deep darkness the peoples; But the Lord will rise upon you, and His glory will appear upon you. And nations will come to your light, and kings to the brightness of your rising" (Isa. 60:1-3). Finally, the prophet Daniel in similar mode predicted that during the time of the end, "those who have insight will shine brightly like the brightness of the expanse of heaven, and those who lead the many to righteousness like the stars forever and ever" (Dan. 12:3). Glorious promises from our King to His followers.

TOWARD FINANCIAL TERRORISM

Henry Morris begins to summarize this time of economic woe in the following manner: "... the overriding characteristic of the world after the third seal is broken is one of violence and near anarchy, along with severe famine and food shortage" (1983, p. 116). In an even more sobering and admittedly controversial argument, John McManus proposed over 20 years ago in the title of his book, Financial Terrorism (1993), that "Debts, deficits, taxation, regulation, and all the other hallmarks of economic slavery are already ravaging this nation. If the designs of those who are plunging America into economic catastrophe aren't blocked – and soon – America's future will resemble what novelist George Orwell had one of his characters forecast in his prophetic 1984 ... 'If you want a picture of the future, imagine a boot stamping on a human face forever.'" (p. 1)

Arguing from a Conspiracy View perspective, McManus and those who agree with him believe that the chief architect of this economic decline are those who wish to ultimately stage a worldwide financial *coup d'etat* by wrenching control of national economies out of local hands and placing them firmly into the hands of a ruling elite in a New World Order. This comports neatly with the plans of the Antichrist to take full military, political and economic control over the nations as he solidifies his power base during his time of rule over the earth. From our present interpretive perspective, this Antichrist will not be revealed until believers are supernaturally removed at a later time, but his spirit will largely define the cultural *zeitgeist,* or spirit and methods of these insidious times.

A Note on Cyber Terror

Still more recently in this now digitalized age of terrorism, multiple Western financial accounts are being targeted by heretofore unidentified actors, intent on bringing the United States to her financial knees through what is now termed, *cyberterrorism* (cf. Berman, 2015; Hayward, 2015). In these increasingly real and threatening scenarios, American companies and government facilities are severely compromised and ultimately disabled, leaving us without the means of meeting our growing financial payments and purchases.

More chilling is the powerful analysis done by law enforcement expert and FBI futurist Mark Goodman, founder and current head of the Future Crimes Institute in California. His compelling book, Future Crimes (2015), says this in the Prologue of a section best described as a gathering techno-storm:

> The subject of this book isn't just what was going on yesterday or even what is happening today. Nor is its focus how long your password should be. It is about where we are going *tomorrow.* In my own research and investigations, first with the LAPD and later working with federal and international law enforcement organizations, I have uncovered criminals who have progressed well beyond today's cybercrime into new and emerging fields of technology such as robotics, virtual reality, artificial intelligence, 3-D printing, and synthetic biology. (p. 2; emph. added)

All this to severely warn of, to use Aldous Huxley's epic title, A Brave New World (1932) that is already all but upon us, about which very, very few of us are aware.

Taken together, these findings and trends demonstrate clearly and alarmingly that as war proliferates, economies decline, prices through hyperinflation increase, and hunger and fear and desperation become more widespread, there will be a heightened interest in two events occurring. One, people will increasingly begin to hoard and prepare for a doomsday of some sort. And two, there will be an increasing desire for a strongman leader who will reestablish order in the midst of intensifying levels of chaos. This is precisely how Adolf Hitler acceded to power in then-Weimar Germany, and how Communism gripped the old Soviet Union for 70 years.

Though admittedly controversial and difficult to prove, McManus (1993) argues that organizations such as the Trilateral Commission and Council on Foreign Relations are part of a global scheme to wrest financial and political control from individual countries and centralize them with the help of the bankers into a One World Government, which will in time become the political and economic infrastructure of the Antichrist system.

McManus goes on to quote Harvard professor and historian Carroll Quigley to define the essential strategy that is presently being employed to achieve these arcane ends. "[T]he powers of financial capitalism had another far-reaching aim, nothing less than to create a world system of financial control in private hands able to dominate the political system of each country and the economy of the world as a whole. This system was to be controlled in a feudalist fashion by the central banks of the world acting in concert, by secret agreements arrived at in frequent private meetings and conferences" (1993, p. 23; cf. Quigley, 1966, p. 324).

Whether or not one agrees with this theory of financial conspiracy, one can easily agree that our financial times are ominous at best, and potentially catastrophic at worst. Thomas Lifson's (2015) warnings, again, are worth reiterating here. In addition, there are thousands of commentaries and blogs today that are predicting that a full-blown Great Depression is in the wings – all of which would serve the dark interests of those who would take advantage of such conditions through the seizing of control over what would be left of a shattered world economy. There are even growing reports predicting that the American government may soon find an excuse to declare martial law in order to restore order to all the social, political, and economic mayhem (Zane, 2014).

And all of this was predicted by the third seal over two thousand years ago. It is my studied view that the birth pangs of this judgment are already evident in the morning newspaper, television or online news sources. The Four Horsemen of the Apocalypse are riding forth, and as the eminent Mr. Graham warned us long ago, we can more and more readily hear their approaching hoof beats. And yet, a fourth horse and rider must be considered before we move toward the true sign of the Lord's Return.

Chapter 6: The Fourth Seal Judgment

It is important to remind at this point that a close reading of the Book of Revelation clearly shows a dramatic intensification of judgments, as we proceed from one to the very next one. Such is the case here, in rather stark relief. So much so that one commentator suggests strongly that this seal "seems to refer to ... the Great Tribulation" (Thames, 2014, p. 56). Not quite so. I remain firmly convinced that again, this period of the seal judgments *precedes* the Wrath of God, and though the section below is stunning in its breadth and power, we are not yet at that place called The Day of the Lord. With that in mind, let us proceed.

THE OPENING OF THE FOURTH SEAL

And when He broke the fourth seal, I heard the voice of the fourth living creature saying, "Come." And I looked, and behold, an ashen horse; and he who sat on it had the name Death; and Hades was following with him. And authority was given to them over a fourth of the earth, to kill with sword and with famine and with pestilence and by the wild beasts of the earth. (Rev. 6:7-8)

An Ashen Horse

I vividly recall a YouTube video recorded and uploaded in February of 2011, in the middle of the so-called Arab Spring, which shows a bloody uprising in Cairo, Egypt back then. As the Euronews cameras captured the mayhem of small arms fire, tanks and the dead and wounded being carried off as part of the arguably American State Department encouraged anti-Mubarek revolt, an extraordinary thing happened, stunning the reporters and viewers alike. What was unmistakably a ghostly rider on a pale green horse advanced straight down the middle of the demonstrations, then calmly rode off and disappeared screen right (cf. "Ghost – Fourth Horseman," 2011).

The Greek rendering in this passage for "pale horse" derives from the Greek word, *chloros*, referring here to an animal that is "sickly pale," or as the very terms describes more literally, "pale or livid as a corpse." Extending these translations, we are to consider this color as that of a *pale green*, as it signifies and accompanies the presence and experience of Death itself. And this concept is taken from the familiar Greek term, *thanatos*, meaning in the context of this alarming passage, "death by violence" as when one is suffering some sort of punishment (Zodhiates, 1990, p. 2183).

Noah Webster's classic dictionary again gives us an up close and linguistically accurate description of this important word that most people fear very deeply:

> That state of a being, animal or vegetable, but more particularly of an animal, in which there is a total and permanent cessation of all the vital functions, when the organs have not only ceased to act, but have lost the susceptibility of renewed action. (1828, Online)

Thus do we have the absolute, clearly violent terminus of human life in this passage, occurring on a massive scale, even unto "a fourth of the earth." By the numbers then, with approximately seven billion souls currently living on the earth, we are talking about no fewer than 1,750,000,000 lives lost in this catastrophic event.

Interestingly, the rider on this pale green horse not only had 'Death' following after him, but also its always troubling companion, Hades. The Greek word used in this New Testament passage is *hades*, rendered as "the place or state of departed souls," as with "the grave, or hell." Spiros Zodhiates gives us a sobering but biblically precise description of this very real region:

> According to the notions of the Hebrews, hades was a vast subterranean receptacle where the souls of the dead existed in a separate state until the resurrection of

their bodies. The region of the blessed during this interval, the inferior paradise, they supposed to be in the upper part of this receptacle; while beneath was the abyss or Gehenna, Tartarus, in which the souls of the wicked were subjected to punishment. (1990, p. 2082)

The staggering implications here cannot be ignored: We shall all be judged at some time during or following The Eschaton. No exceptions. And this ought to give each of us sober pause indeed about our life now, and the Life (or Death) yet to come. Or as the ancient Hebrews would advise and I am often seen to state it: Selah.

A Précis on Hell

Perhaps the most deeply disturbing concept in all of human experience is the idea of an eternal, fiery Hell, where all the wicked shall yet end up. Now the following is not meant as biblical canon, but rather the result of a recent and quite thorough exploration into the biblical passages that clearly, in my studied view, tell us which individuals go to Hell, and just what shall be their experience of it. So bear with me as I propose here several ideas concerning what I have only recently termed, the *Traditionalist-Conditionalist View of Hell.*

There are two leading theological views of the concept of Hell, the Traditionalist, and the more recent, Conditionalist (see an accurate summary of these competing perspectives in a reprint of James Kenneth Brandyberry's pioneering work in Gregg, 2013). On one side of this ageless argument is the *Traditionalist View of Hell* that has for centuries taught us the orthodox view that all evil people outside of a faith in God shall descend into a fiery place of eternal torment, that again virtually all cultures conceive of as Hell writ very large and torturous. On the other side is the more recent *Conditionalist View of Hell*, in which those not "in Christ" for eternal life simply die, or are annihilated in the biblical "second death" at the Judgment, rather than suffer forever (Rev. 20:14).

While I could quote numerous Scriptures to describe this idea, I'll stay with the Book of Revelation given the context of this study. Chapter 21, verse 8 for example, says this:

> But for the cowardly and unbelieving and abominable and murderers and immoral persons and sorcerers and idolaters and all liars, their part will be in the lake that burns with fire and brimstone, which is the second death.

Not much wiggle room here. Sinners clearly named. The "lake that burns with fire and brimstone" (eternally, by the way). But wait, there is also the phrase, "the second death," and that is where I dove into the Old and New Testament Scriptures to find out just what this meant, what John the Apostle meant and what Jesus the Revelator meant.

We have already defined, by both biblical account and the brilliant Christian lexicographer Noah Webster what Death is: The End. Thus is built in here the idea, yes the unmistakable idea, that for some, at least, the eternal Lake of Fire completely *consumes* these evildoers, as with the phrase with which most of us are intimately familiar, "Our God is a consuming fire" (cf. Dt. 4:24; Heb. 12:29). Now stay with me here. Jude 13 similarly describes a place of "black darkness" (or "nether gloom") where these wicked shall go, similar to Jesus' own declaration that such people will be cast into "outer darkness," where there shall be "weeping and gnashing of teeth" (Mt. 25:30).

So what's my point? Just this. I am beginning to consider that the mass of the unbelievers in this world will indeed descend into that fiery place called Hell, but possibly at least, not to be tormented forever, but rather to experience indeed the Second Death, or Annihilation, to be utterly and finally consumed in the complete *destruction* of the body and soul, as Jesus Himself proclaimed in Matthew 10:28. The Greek term used by the Lord there is *apollumi*, which by any rendering means, "destroy fully, perish, die, lose life, render void," in this context, eternally.

Now before you run to incinerate this passage and book for its possible heretical departure (I prefer orthodox refinement, if you please) from the Traditional View of Hell, now watch this, as Charles Stanley would caution. Go back to Revelation, and read closely, closely now, this otherwise well-worn passage:

> And the devil who deceived them was thrown into the lake of fire and brimstone, where the beast and the false prophet are also; and <u>they</u> will be *tormented day and night forever and ever.* (20:10; emph. added)

Well now. We have always been taught that Hell was originally constructed by God as an "eternal fire prepared for the devil and his angels" (Mt. 25:41). Roger that. So combined with this passage from Revelation, it is arguably possible, at the very least, that Hell is still and only intended for: the Devil, his angels, the Beast (or Antichrist), and the False Prophet.

But what of all those humans who are supposed to join them? Now here is where I humbly submit that I experienced a bit of an epiphany while discussing all this with a dear brother in Romania recently. I was led to reread very carefully this lengthy passage that combines with the others like a well-fitting glove, the manner of all Scripture which cannot contradict itself. Ever.

> And another angel, a third one, followed them, saying with a loud voice, "If anyone worships the beast and his image, and receives a mark on his forehead or upon his hand, he also will drink of the wine of the wrath of God, which is mixed in full strength in the cup of His anger; and he will be tormented with fire and brimstone in the presence of the holy angels and in the presence of the Lamb. And the smoke of their torment goes up forever and ever; and *<u>they</u> have no rest day and night,* those

who worship the beast and his image, and whoever receives the mark of his name." (Rev. 14:9-11; emph. added)

I tell you true, when I reread this powerful section of Scripture, I fairly fell out of my chair. If I have this right, only those who "worship the beast and his image," and who concomitantly "receive a mark on his or her forehead or on the hand" will be tormented in that same Lake of Fire built for the Devil, his angels, the Beast, and the False Prophet.

And if so, we have one Lake of Fire that burns eternally, but *two destinies* for the wicked, as it were. For the commonplace unsaved, there is reserved for them the Conditionalist, Second Death, or Annihilation, the end of existence forever, as they are consumed by that fiery place upon entering it. But for those who not only reject God but also bow down to his Ancient Foe, Satan, and end up bowing down also to his emissary, the Antichrist or Beast and his False Prophet, and demonic agents or "angels," there is the more Traditionalist conception of a special fiery punishment stored up for them, that lasts indeed forever and ever and ever, as they are consumed in an altogether different and more horrendous way.

And if any of this slight heterodoxy becomes injurious to God's Truth in any way, I shall quickly and quite publicly depart from it. But I must say again that I sensed that I was to present this here, in this section, as spiritual food for great thought in the distressing days ahead. One thing is certain, whether or not I am correct in these assessments: Love God, love Truth and love His people with all your might; and have absolutely nothing to do with Satan and his lies or his evil emissaries, no matter what. And once more I say: Selah.

The Various Means of Death

The rest of this compelling passage begins with the declaration that this Rider was given "authority" to take peace from a fourth of the earth, as I mentioned earlier. The Greek word used here for such power is, *exousia,* which translates as "force, capacity, competency, freedom, mastery, delegated influence, jurisdiction, right, or strength" (Zodhiates, 1990, p. 2166). Thus in this context it refers to the raw, Divine power indeed to wreak havoc on a quarter of the planet, which will plough through the nations with Death and Hell on its violent heels.

The first means of such deadly mayhem is the *sword.* Without much need for exegesis here, clearly the Scriptures are referring to violence and War writ large, as with the Red Horse and Rider who brought war to some of the earth in the Second Seal. So now the massive proliferation of wars come to a much broader scale of our planet, well beyond the mere "rumors" of wars proclaimed by the Messiah (Mt. 24:6; Mk. 13:7). Now we are in the thick of it, with rapidly increasing expansion of mortal conflicts among and between the nations.

And of course the first thing that comes to mind are the mounting threats of militant Islam against the West in their avowed historic goal to construct that worldwide Caliphate referenced earlier in which all must bend a knee to Allah, or die a horrific death (refer to earlier sections on Islam for details). Or conceivably via an attack by China or Russia, both of whom are in increasingly cooperative coalition with each other and with Islam, and the rapid mulitplication of their respective military might and war machines (cf. Grant, 2011, p. 9; Ezek. 38-39).

The second means of Death here is another wave of judgment we described earlier: *Famine.* Noah Webster's rendering again deserves emphasis to precisely define this inconceivable condition: "Scarcity of food; dearth; a general want of provisions sufficient for the inhabitants of a country or besieged place ... [Severe] Want; destitution" (1828, online). Most of us cannot imagine the power of famine, unless we turn once more to still another grisly passage from Scripture to drive home its terrors:

> Then you shall eat the offspring of your own body, the flesh of your sons and of your daughters whom the LORD your God has given you, during the siege and the distress by which your enemy will oppress you. The man who is refined and very delicate among you shall be hostile toward his brother and toward the wife he cherishes and toward the rest of his children who remain, so that he will not give *even* one of them any of the flesh of his children which he will eat, since he has nothing *else* left, during the siege and the distress by which your enemy will oppress you in all your towns. (Deut. 28:53-55)

Thus do the siege works of war and violent calamity surge forth upon the earth to such a degree that humanity begins to devour its own, even its children, in order to survive. And this is not yet the Wrath of God, but the angers of Satan and the disobedient depravity of Man in toxic alliance prior to the Day of the Lord.

And finally there is this rather mysterious section. In the spirit of full disclosure, my wife and I turn to our SyFy cable channel for some oftentimes comic relief in the forms of Sharknado, Dinoshark, Atomic Shark, Ice Shark, several Mega-Shark tales, or Ice Spiders, Franken Fish, Flu Bird Horror, Scream of the Banshee and other sundry, non-Oscar offerings. While we may chuckle at such nonsense, I came to the conclusion long ago that God speaks through strange channels indeed. Thus it is possible that even here we see harbingers of things to come, and here's why.

The final means by which Death visits a fourth of the earth here is found through unprecedented attacks by *wild beasts* of the earth. Of course theologians fight even over this straight forward description of what the Greek term *therion,* which neatly translates as, well, "wild beasts" or animals such as the wolf, or the lion, or, yes with some apology, the ever fearsome shark. Also implied are those creatures that are "venomous," and by extension, the equally clear implication that we will enter upon a time when we shall increasingly be required "to fight with wild beasts" in order, again, to survive (Zodhiates, 1990, p. 2186).

As one trained in scientific method during my doctoral studies days, I later learned as a Christian that good science and sound theology are not in competition with one another as we are so often taught. With that in mind, Marc Lallanilla (2014) calmly and reasonably describes why there is a spike in animal attacks on humans, including such natural factors as increased scarcity of food sources, restriction and reduction of their territorial hunting grounds and so on. All of which will intensify during the Seal Judgments.

In sum, we must consider the progressive intensification of these early judgments as we proceed from the going forth of the Antichrist to consolidate his political power around the world, combined with his sponsorship of wars of both the international and internecine types. Of special note is the latter kind which we find more and more right here in the United States, as Class War is increasingly evident between political factions, racial and economic groups, and even in the midst of Liberal and Conservative ideological constituencies. Everywhere it seems, *deep Division* is the case, even it would appear, between species. Historically significant to our times are the words of Jesus: "If a house is divided against itself, that house will not be able to stand." (Mk. 3:25) Still again: Selah.

So now we turn to an even more troubling development for what the prophet Mohammed called, "People of the Book" in the Fifth Seal judgment. Both Christians and Jews are to be most severely forewarned that an even greater darkness is coming to many of those who call God their Lord. And many would argue, is already begun.

Chapter 7: The Fifth Seal Judgment

For a number of reasons, some known to me but others not, I have for the past two to three years been pondering the question if I would be able to die for Jesus Christ, if called upon to do so. No answers yet by the way. But in all that pondering, I am coming to terms with an Ultimate Question: How much am I willing to lay down for following God? I think it is a question that comes to each of us at least once in our lives of living The Faith. And for the purposes of this book and especially this chapter, it is a question that will burn more brightly in the years just ahead, if I am discerning the times accurately. The Fifth Seal takes us to this place where a certain number of us shall yet travel.

THE OPENING OF THE FIFTH SEAL

And when he broke the fifth seal, I saw underneath the altar the souls of those who had been slain because of the word of God, and because of the testimony which they had maintained; and they cried out with a loud voice, saying, "How long, O Lord, holy and true, wilt Thou refrain from judging and avenging our blood on those who dwell on the earth?" And there was given to each of them a white robe; and they were told that they should rest for a little while longer, until the number of their fellow servants and their brethren who were to be killed even as they had been, would be completed also. (Rev. 6:9-11)

The entire history of Christianity and the Church has been marked by several signatures, not the least of which is **persecution**. Christ Himself predicted this would be the case during His time on this earth, and the reasons why in this well-known passage: "If the world hates you, realize that it hated Me first. If you belonged to the world, the world would love its own; but because you do not belong to the world, and I have chosen you out of the world, the world hates you" (Jn. 15:18-19). Thus are we to expect persecution to some degree, in exact proportion to the degree we are like Him, in thought, word and deed.

The Greek word for "hate" in the above passage is *miseo*, translated as "to hate, pursue with hatred, detest, to be hated, detested or otherwise loved less than all others;" ergo, to be severely persecuted often without reason (Zodhiates, 1990, p. 2224). Thus are we who believe in the God of the Bible to anticipate being shown various degrees and forms of hostility, ill-treatment, and even oppression especially because of our religious beliefs. While we in the United States have enjoyed the historic freedom found in the First Amendment to worship and express our beliefs openly, today such freedoms are under assault more than ever before.

Many leading conservative and Christian scholars wrote long ago of such hostility as part of our national decline, and the larger decline of the West. Mirroring the thinking of distinguished lawyer, Lutheran theologian, and professor John Warwick Montgomery alluded to in an earlier chapter, these authors believe that the nation and the world are in steep decline, or to restate the phrase used by British historian Paul Johnson again, experiencing unprecedented *degringolade,* defined as the rapid deterioration or downfall in strength, position or condition (1983, Ch. 7). While one may debate that claim on the historic merits, clearly there is a sense that something is wrong with America and the nations today, that we are pitched upon the edge of that dangerous precipice eloquently described, again, by Jewish philosopher Gertrude Himmelfarb (1994).

It is the thesis of this book and rendering that such decline is a major cause of increased persecution of God's people, since a departure from biblical faith runs in lockstep with hatred and animosity toward the people of God. The calculus here is inarguable, as illustrated in Alexander

Solzhenitsyn's seismic Harvard University declaration that America's demise is due to her having forgotten God (1978). Despised at the time for such bold critique from a Russian, no less, his diagnosis today seems all too painfully prescient and precise. Thus we now turn to our biblical description of the Fifth Seal in that context, that portends that members of faith communities will suffer persecution and even death to the degree that a nation forgets or rejects the God of Scripture.

The Slain Souls

We see in Revelation 6 verse 9 a description of a number of "souls of those who had been slain" because of their belief in the Bible and their open testimony to His Word and to Him. The word for "slain" here is instructive of course, taken from the Greek word, *sphazo*, meaning to slay, kill by violence, slaughter, wound mortally; i.e., to butcher (Zodhiates, 1990, p. 2286). Terrifying to most of us of course, this is the fate of a relatively *limited* number of believers in this pre-Wrath period of early tremors. I say "limited" since these martyrs are to be distinguished from the massive numbers who will be slain, mostly by beheadings, in the Tribulation Era which follows (cf. Rev. 7:14, 19; 13:7; 20:4).

Lest we lose heart at such contemplations, let us not again forget the blood-soaked history of the Church (and the Jews I quickly add here), the former heralded in the deeply moving classic, John Foxe's Book of Martyrs (1563). This, an historic chronicle of the savage persecutions of Christians beginning in the ancient world, and proceeding through his own times in Catholic Scotland and England. Here is an example of the tortures that many suffered under the Roman dictator Nero around AD 67:

> This dreadful conflagration continued nine days; when Nero, finding that his conduct was greatly blamed, and a severe odium cast upon him, determined to lay the whole upon the Christians, at once to excuse himself,

and have an opportunity of glutting his sight with new cruelties. This was the occasion of the first persecution; and the barbarities exercised on the Christians were such as even excited the commiseration of the Romans themselves. Nero even refined upon cruelty, and contrived all manner of punishments for the Christians that the most infernal imagination could design. In particular, he had some sewed up in skins of wild beasts, and then worried by dogs until they expired; and others dressed in shirts made stiff with wax, fixed to axletrees, and set on fire in his gardens, in order to illuminate them. This persecution was general throughout the whole Roman Empire; but it rather increased than diminished the spirit of Christianity. In the course of it, St. Paul and St. Peter were martyred. (Ch. II)

Today of course, we cannot imagine such horrors, unless of course you happen to be born in many Islamic-controlled nations in the Middle East, as introduced earlier.

A second element we see in the Fifth Seal passage is that this group of martyrs cried out with a loud voice for God's judgments and even for His "avenging" their blood on those who still dwelled on the earth (v. 10). Now most of us have been taught that such a prayer contravenes the teachings of Jesus, since we are to love our enemies, and bless and pray for those who persecute us (e.g., Mt. 5:44). But again, we cannot understand the passage in Revelation unless we take a precise look at the words used here, particularly the one used for "avenging." Taken from the Greek term, *ekdikeo*, it indicates a strong request for justice through, or defense of, as with vindication. Or as Zodhiates renders it, to "retaliate, punish, or maintain one's right and make penal satisfaction" (1990, p. 2154).

In all of this then, this group does not cry out so much for vengeance, but rather God's proper and measured response to their suffering, the same sort of plea we too often hear these days when a family member is slain by a rogue criminal who must appear before a legitimate magistrate for sentencing. It is at core, a fervent plea for *justice* in the final analysis, for as the Scriptures thankfully proclaim, our God is a God of justice, who loves justice, without which the universe would be a bloodier still cacophony of anarchism and lawlessness. Or as the prophet Isaiah says it plainly: "For I, the LORD, love justice [or 'proper claim, rectitude']" (61:8).

More to the present (and future) point, the world is fast entering upon that rapid decline into what Jesus described as a time of intensifying *lawlessness,* during which time the love of multitudes will grow cold (Mt. 24:12). The Greek word here for lawlessness is, significantly, *anomia,* meaning illegality, violation, wickedness, iniquity, and unrighteousness (Zodhiates, 1990, p. 2100). It reminds me quickly of a term I examined during my doctoral studies as presented by French social theorist Emile Durkheim, who described a time of rampant "Anomie," or a state of being experienced vastly more by the irreligious than the religious, resulting in rapid increases of the title of his now classic work, *Le Suicide* (1897). This tragic truth is found among those who neither knew Joseph nor Jesus, as I personally found out on October 30, 1979 when I had planned to take my own life. You may recall my touching upon that event in the Foreward of this book (cf. Exod. 1:8; Jn. 3:16).

We finish this passage with what has always struck me as a mystery of sorts. The text describes this group of martyrs (or sufferers for the cause of Christ) as dressed out in "white robes" signifying their righteousness according to virtually all commentaries. But then this: They are commanded to rest "for a little while longer, until *the number of* their fellow servants and their brethren" are to be killed (v. 11; emph. added). The New American Standard text italicizes this phrase, as an index for a strongly implied meaning, though not literally found in the original biblical texts. But then what can this mean for those of us who are now alive and, as I argue, moving through this dangerous period?

Just this, in my studied view. Our God is a God of precision who I have become convinced loves numbers. Big time. I recall delving into the richness of this biblical literature during my years at Regent University in Virginia, as I perused the fascinating pages of a book titled, Numbers in the Bible: God's Unique Design in Biblical Numbers by Robert D. Johnston (1990). All that to say that I propose that this passage clearly shows that there is, in the Mind of God, *a specific number* of martyrs who are to be slain, before God's Wrath is poured out on those who killed them. Note that this seal is coming up just this side of the Sixth Seal, when as I shall argue the full Anger of God appears on the scene. This proximity is not to be lost on the reader.

A Further Note on Our Present Perils

As I conclude this section, I would be remiss to not mention two sources of increased dangers for American Christians. The first has to do with domestic policy and condition, and the second with foreign policy and events. Here at home, there is ample evidence in our daily news that persecution is on the rapid increase. In the highly regarded journal, American Thinker, award winning, Princeton-educated theologian Fay Voshell describes such persecution increasing in stages, arguing that we are now in at least the initial stages of such ignominy. She writes:

> The first stage begins with attempts to stereotype the targeted group. Our current president [Obama] summed up the Christian-hating left's views of people of faith when in 2008, he categorized working-class voters in the following way: "[I]t's not surprising, then, that they get bitter, they cling to guns or religion or antipathy to people who aren't like them or anti-immigrant sentiment

or anti-trade sentiment as a way to explain their frustrations." (2015, para. 5)

In her clear indictment of the political Left in this country, she also quotes Hard Ball journalist Chris Matthews, an arguably liberal Catholic himself, who tweeted this: "If you're a politician and believe in God first, that's all good. Just don't run for government office, run for church office" (para. 15).

On the foreign policy side and field, no one can deny, again, that militant Islam and ISIS and Iran in particular, are on a bloody march against both Christians and Jews, the Great Satan America and the Little Satan Israel. No need to document atrocities here, save for more insight from another American Thinker piece that aptly sums up this historic crisis. Which in its turn reminds of the ancient wisdom of Chinese military strategist Sun Tzu, who wrote, "If you know the enemy and know yourself, your victory will not stand in doubt; if you know Heaven and know Earth, you may make your victory complete" (The Art of War, c. 500 BC, 2017).

In that penetrating light, here is what journalist William A. Levinson writes, starting with a quote from General George S. Patton:

> General Patton said, "It is difficult to make our fine American youth understand that the enemy wants to kill him ... I use the language of soldiers who are ready to kill." It is similarly difficult to make Euro-Americans understand that certain people who call themselves Muslims want to kill our civilization, our society and our way of life. The power to name a thing is the power to control or destroy it and, if we are afraid to so much as name the enemy, we are helpless against him. (May 31, 2013, para. 2)

Thus the president's abject refusal during his entire administration to name the enemy for what and who it is – Orthodox Islam – catastrophically prevents the United States from martialing our forces against this dreaded foe, since it runs Gen. Tzu's recommendations straight into the ground. Thus we remain in greater peril than most of us realize.

So do I conclude this section on a somewhat somber and intensely personal note concerning the souls among us who will face death by a domestic or foreign foe in years to come. I wonder at times: If called on, *am I willing* to lay down my life for Christ? And yet, there are for the believer at least two overarching Hopes that gird us for such times. One captured by the brilliant poet, John Donne in his Holy Sonnet X, and the other by another, equally gifted writer, Dylan Thomas.

Both are odes to dying well in the Lord, encouragement to us all who may face such a day. Or night. First, Mr. Donne:

> Death, be not proud, though some have called thee
> Mighty and dreadful, for thou are not so;
> For those whom thou think'st thou dost overthrow
> Die not, poor Death, nor yet canst thou kill me.
> From rest and sleep, which but thy pictures be,
> Much pleasure; then from thee much more must flow,
> And soonest our best men with thee do go,
> Rest of their bones, and soul's delivery.
>
> Thou'art slave to fate, chance, kings, and desperate men,
> And dost with poison, war, and sickness dwell,
> And poppy'or charms can make us sleep as well
> And better than thy stroke; why swell'st thou then?
> One short sleep past, we wake eternally,
> And death shall be no more; Death, thou shalt die.
> (1609)

And next on a more militant note, one that I personally favor to be honest, from Mr. Thomas:

Do not go gentle into that good night,
Old age should burn and rage at close of day;
Rage, rage against the dying of the light.

Though wise men at their end know dark is right,
Because their words had forked no lightning they
Do not go gentle into that good night.

Good men, the last wave by, crying how bright
Their frail deeds might have danced in a green bay,
Rage, rage against the dying of the light.

Wild men who caught and sang the sun in flight,
And learn, too late, they grieved it on its way,
Do not go gentle into that good night.

Grave men, near death, who see with blinding sight
Blind eyes could blaze like meteors and be gay,
Rage, rage against the dying of the light.

And you, my father, there on the sad height,
Curse, bless me now with your fierce tears, I pray.
Do not go gentle into that good night.
Rage, rage against the dying of the light. (1951)

So may the Most High God prepare all who are about to die in Him and for Him to choose well which course to follow, should we be called to such high privilege.

Chapter 8: The Sixth Seal Judgment

Now we come to a place in Scripture and world history where human language and comprehension frankly fail, for the events that I shall now attempt to describe are for all intents and purposes beyond words, both literally and figuratively. Thus did the Apostle John on the stark landscapes and caves of Patmos likely struggle all the more to record what Jesus the Revelator was showing him. And thus do I struggle in my own efforts here to paint a verbal portrait of what I can only label as an epochal, **Cosmic Shift** – from the world as we know it, to a world as it is about to become for the very first and only time in all of human history. Or as one writer put it concerning one of the opening salvo of the Sixth Seal, "*it is the shaking of the Universe*" that occurs here, and nothing less (Thames, 2014, p. 57; cf. Hag. 2:5-7; emph. added).

In staggering sum, thus commences what we have written of earlier as *The Day of the Lord*, that time of which all the ancients wrote as the beginning of **God's Wrath,** burning hotter than ever before in all the annals of the human race. As this massive Shaking descends upon the earth then, the ages and epochs now shatter and break, much as the tectonic plates beneath the continents begin to divide, fold and then burst forth with devastation almost impossible to describe, again, in human terms.

Grasp that, and you begin to understand this massive transfer from one Era to Another, described by most biblical superscripts by a single term: **Terror.**

THE OPENING OF THE SIXTH SEAL

[12]I looked when He broke the sixth seal, and there was a great earthquake; and the sun became black as sackcloth made of hair, and the whole moon became like blood; [13]and the stars of the sky fell to the earth, as a fig tree casts its unripe figs when shaken by a great wind. [14]The sky was split apart like a scroll when it is

rolled up, and every mountain and island were moved out of their places. Then the kings of the earth and the great men and the commanders and the rich and the strong and every slave and free man hid themselves in the caves and among the rocks of the mountains; and they said to the mountains and to the rocks, "Fall on us and hide us from the presence of Him who sits on the throne, and from the wrath of the Lamb; for the great day of their wrath has come, and who is able to stand?" (Rev. 6:12-17)

Please note, that unique to this Seal alone, I have chosen to leave the numeric designations for each verse intact, in order to more accurately track the progression of these startling events.

A Great Earthquake

In verse 12 then, we see the breaking forth of a "great" quake, the scale of which I alluded to above: An unprecedented, massive, and horrifying shaking of the entire earth, all the heavens and the total Cosmos. Various writers described its power so great, that it "shook land and sea, and the very starry heavens were thrown into disorder." Virtually impossible to conceive, Dr. Steve Austin of the Institute for Creation Research writes that it will be none other than "God's voice" that will thunder 'cross the entire Universe to bring such a shaking (2010). But one other view by the brilliant geological scientist, anthropologist and student of the ancient texts, Dr. Jeffrey Goodman, brings much of this home for us.

Of his increasingly widely and highly regarded, The Comets of God (2010), Dr. Bethe Hagans, Professor of Anthropology at Walden University wrote: "You make an ingenious case for your belief that [almost] all large-scale phenomena described or prophesied in the Bible can be explained as a consequence of known phenomena, notably comets" (as cited in Goodman, 2011, Back Cover). Concerning this possibility is a somewhat obscure notation in the work of mathematician Taylor A. Cisco, Jr. in All Shall Hide (2010), which proposes: "This scripture may pertain to violent ground shocks that may be caused by a meteoroid impact" (p. 3).

In the compelling introduction of his well-researched thesis, Goodman observes: "The descriptions of the end times impact events found in the Book of Revelation are consistent with Job 38:22-23 (NIV). The 'storehouses of the snow' and the 'storehouses of the hail' are actually the comets of the Oort Cloud the God of the Bible says He has 'reserved for the times of trouble, for days of battle and war'" (2010, pp. 195-196). While most of this *cosmic mayhem* will occur beginning with the Trumpet and Bowl Judgments of later chapters in that Book, we may surmise for now that comets may also play a role in the disasters pouring forth from the Sixth Seal Judgment, including the massive earthquake described thus at its outset, as Divine Announcement that more supernatural terror is yet to come.

The Sun Becomes Black

Most of us of course are familiar with full solar eclipses, so at first glance this may not seem outside of any ordinary event known to us in the present Age. But as this second catastrophe breaks forth, uniquely, *across the entire earth*, one writer says this of *the entire sun* turning "black as sackcloth made of [goat's] hair" (v. 12): "Because of the dust and gases from the billows of smoke exploding from the earth's core, it will screen and reflect light away from the sun, making it appear to John, again, like black sackcloth made of goat hair (Isaiah 50:3)" (Mack, 2015, para. 3).

The Hebrew term in the Isaiah passage referenced above is *qadruwth*, meaning to make very dark, or as one rendering put it, a darkness associated with a deep "gloom" that befalls the planet. Turning once again to our friend Noah Webster, this term refers to such things as "Obscurity; partial or total darkness; thick shade; as the gloom of a forest, or the gloom of midnight; Cloudiness or heaviness of mind; melancholy; aspect of sorrow. We say, the mind is sunk into gloom; a gloom overspreads the mind; Darkness of prospect or aspect, Sullenness" (1828). Thus it is not inconceivable that in the wake of these first two terror-inspiring events, a great emotional and spiritual *darkness or depression of mind* envelops earth's inhabitants, as they agonize over what is taking place as the lights, both literally and figuratively, go completely out.

The Moon Becomes Like Blood

By some contrast, it is not difficult at all to understand the moon "becoming like blood" from the titanic eruptions on the earth, as Taylor Cisco observed concerning a darkened sun, as masses of dust and gas are blasted into the atmosphere (2010, p. 38). I recall vividly during a trip to Acapulco, Mexico to present a paper in May 1980, when at the same time Mt. St. Helens exploded. The resultant eruption column rose 80,000 feet into the air, and became fully visible in 11 states. I remember well today that as I gazed at the sunsets back then, the colors were a remarkable blend of orange and yellow and red, as the moon indeed became the hue of a blood-like red.

More recently, a wave of fascination and considerable controversy has occurred over something evangelists, pastors and Bible scholars refer to as *Blood Moons* (cf. Biltz, 2014; Hitchcock, 2014). While one may certainly debate the theological and scientific merits of these competing frameworks to explain the cosmic significance and impact of our "whole moon [becoming] like blood" (verse 12), it is in fact going to occur in greatly magnified scope and impact in this Seal Judgment. Thus we must attempt at least, to come to terms with what is happening at this point, in order to further comprehend the times in which it appears on the scene.

Journalist Leo Hohmann gives us a superb overview of these matters, as he writes for World News Daily, a conservative and largely religiously informed news site (2015). The Blood Moon Tetrad idea in previous publications noted above predicts that each of four solar eclipses on April 15 2014, October 8 2014, April 4 2015, and the last occurring on September 28 2015 also fell, arguably for the first time, on four Jewish feasts, respectively – Passover, Sukkot, and then Passover and Sukkot again. The premise here is that God is sending these possibly unprecedented Blood Moons as "signs" of imminent judgment or for those more optimistic, redemption of God's people.

Rabbi Amram Vaknin is featured in Hohmann's piece, as "a mystic rabbi in southern Israel" who urges all Jews to pray and repent as the third and fourth Blood Moons appear. Vaknin predicts that "the 44th President [of the United States, Barack Hussein Obama] would bring bloodshed to the Jewish people," a prophecy he made before Mr. Obama was elected President. These concerns about the American President become all the more salient, these advocates of the Blood Moons argue, since America struck a "Deal" with Iran regarding the Islamic Republic's future nuclear capability. Iran of course is Israel's arch-foe who has sworn repeatedly to annihilate Israel and the United States.

Behind much of this thinking is the work of still another controversial figure, Rabbi Jonathan Cahn, author of the NY Times best-seller, The Mystery of the Shemitah (2014) and other books. As Hohmann (2015) summarizes this widely popular book's thesis: "[Cahn] has also issued warnings that a time of judgment is coming to America and the world in the form of possible stock market collapses and wars" which the Blood Moon Tetrad phenomena foretell, say its advocates. Finally, it is noted that the Hebrew Talmud discusses the significance of astronomical events in human history, specifically stating that solar eclipses are a "warning to the nations, while a lunar eclipse signifies danger for the Jewish people, who are likened to the moon."

The Stars of the Sky Fall to Earth

As catastrophe mounts in the ripping open of the Sixth Seal, we now see that the very stars in the heavens begin to cascade to the earth in, I will safely presume, vast numbers and resulting devastation from their many impacts – "as a fig tree casts its unripe figs when shaken by a great wind" (v. 12). As I reviewed this section, I could not help but look to a degree of solid science to help me understand what the Apostle John could not possibly comprehend. Thus did I turn again to the superb analysis by Dr. Goodman, for some rich insights here, and for the stupendous sections following.

In his Preface to the exceptional book, The Comets of God (2010), Goodman writes the following as part of his basic thesis and premise for understanding apocalyptic literature:

> We find that the catastrophic events recounted in the Bible show that God works through the laws of nature (which he says he established) by using comets as his instruments to implement some of his plans. Readers will be surprised to learn that the Bible refers to comets as God's "mighty ones," "weapons of wrath," and "ministers of flaming fire." Some of God's plans include God revealing himself to mankind via comets, and God bringing correction and judgment via comets. (p. xi)

While Dr. Goodman and I might differ on some of the details concerning the various sequences of judgments in Revelation, we fully concur on this: That comets (in the Greek, *aster*, or falling stars, asteroids, meteorites etc.) play a key role in virtually all of the startling and devastating events in this important system of prophecies.

Goodman then accurately describes the cumulative effect of such a cosmic bombardment, which will very possibly cause the "great earthquake" described in verses 12, 14 and in the final portions of the Sixth Seal events. He goes on to predict that "Dust will be rising into the atmosphere so that it blackens the sun and reddens the moon," as described in the 12th verse as well. This is the result and consequence of the great shaking of, again, not only the earth, but of the very heavens as well. Thus shall come forth that clearly under-appreciated, massive, worldwide "great wind" (v. 13) that scatters dust and debris in every direction on the entire planet, as humanity begins to scramble in terror to understand what is taking place. (p. 360)

The Sky Splits Apart

Of all the Sixth Seal judgments, this is the one that I have struggled with for over 30 years, to begin to understand both the wonder, and yes, the cosmic-rending physics of such an event. That is, the earth's very *skies splitting apart* (v. 13; Isa. 34:4). And no, I do not view this (or other passages in the Seal Judgments) as somehow symbolic or allegorical. That path has been worn far too thin to no good outcome by many Bible scholars who choose to virtually deconstruct prophetic Scriptures here and elsewhere (cf. Ch. 2 re: Preterist, Historicist, and Idealist hermeneutics). So do I venture forth with Dr. Goodman again, aided and abetted by another scientist, Dr. Henry Morris of the Institute for Creation Research, to attempt to explain and visualize this stunning event.

Though not intended to endorse either the Young Earth or Old Earth view of Creation, here is Dr. Morris' (1983) take on this matter. One possibility involves massive clouds of dust spreading across all the skies over the entire earth, making it appear as if it were being rolled up like a scroll. But he quickly adds that it may otherwise result from such powerful and simultaneous, worldwide continental shifts that it would appear that the skies were "departing" or splitting apart, depending on the translation used. But on closer examination of the Greek term used for "split apart" (*apochorizo*), we are talking here about a literal, vicious departure, or "ripping apart," of the very firmament. This of course staggers one's imagination, the known laws of physics, and human credulity.

Thus Dr. Goodman tries this as possible explanation. He writes that these events accumulate to cause "shock waves from the impacts [of comets] causing the atmosphere to roll back" (2010, p. 357). Thus it is, quite literally and catastrophically, that the firmament is torn apart and rolled back! But even this leaves us a bit short on understanding, again, the natural forces of such a catastrophe. But this much is clear to me: Somehow the inhabitants of the earth watch the very skies "depart" in such a way that they will be able to catch a terrifying glimpse of the larger Reality of what is about to descend on the earth, the result of which is once more, unmitigated, unprecedented Terror. And the key to that glimpse is found in the final three verses of this epic prophecy.

Finally, then, we see even more that every mountain and island are moved out of their places. But now look again: That is *every* mountain and *every* island are displaced from their natural location and stability (v. 14). As one who grew up in the midst of South California where earthquakes are common occurrences, I cannot nonetheless conceive of this sort of raw, bone-rattling power shaking all that we take for granted as unmovable and unshakable. And if ever there were a symbolic meaning here, that is precisely it: God is clearly *shaking the nations* out of all their presumptions of security, to shout for our attentions that He and He alone is our only Safe Harbor.

The Onset of Divine Terror

As the peoples of the earth reel to and fro under the combined ravages of the earth and its entire crust splitting, cracking, folding and shaking beneath them, comets and meteors crashing to the ground causing fiery devastation everywhere, and what appears to be ripping apart of the skies above, they begin to cascade into what would conceivably become a worldwide, cacophonous, ear and mind shattering, **chaotic panic.** Thus do the leaders (kings and great men and women), the rich and the poor alike, those in places of strength and security alongside those who are weak, penniless and even under various forms of oppression, literally and frantically look for places to hide. They even run for any caves or underground shelter carved from rocks to escape what is occurring (v. 15).

In fact, there is a gathering, terrified sense here that virtually all classes of society are seized with unprecedented, collective panic. As they more and more comprehend that God is pouring out *His Wrath,* they run to the caves and among the rocks of the mountains or anywhere they can find shelter from the ecological chaos literally raining down from heaven. Indeed, here they much prefer to be crushed by tumbling mountains and rocks than to endure the severe Angers of Almighty God – who they now recognize is not a Myth after all. So now do we come to that Epochal Moment in history when all Mankind, for the first time in that history, begins to more fully grasp what is going on.

I turn now to the literal presentation of that Moment, as recorded by John the Apostle:

> [A]nd they said to the mountains and to the rocks, "Fall on us and hide us from the presence of [or lit., 'face'] *of Him who sits on the throne, and from the wrath of the Lamb."* (v. 16)

Several astounding facts are here revealed. First and foremost, again, the world finally "gets it," that God is Ruler of all, and that He is not happy. Why do they know this? Because the skies have been rolled back in part, for them to catch a glimpse of His fiery "Presence," or by the Greek rendering from *prosopon*, they are permitted to see the very Face of the Godhead in all His fury. Thus do they, *en masse*, quite literally melt in that fiery Presence, as they in one instant comprehend that the ravages of both Hell and Heaven are come full and furious to the earth, as permitted and ordained by its Governor in Heaven.

Note secondly that the Trinity is in some evidence here, since the peoples of the earth see the One who sits on the throne (the Heavenly Father; cf. Rev. 4:2; 5:13; 21:5). But they simultaneously see The Lamb of God, who we know is always found "at the right hand of the Father" (cf. Mk. 16:19; Acts 7:55). And once again, the context of this entire passage makes crystal, terrifyingly clear that God is undeniably enraged at this point, having been taken to all His divine limits in witnessing the mounting waves of sin cascading across the whole earth, even among the nations He had to that point favored. Think here of all the formerly Christian nations of Europe and yes, so tragically, the United States of America.

So to the core thesis of this work, as a great cry issues forth from all Humanity: "[For] the great day of **Their [or His] Wrath** has come; and who is able to stand?" (v. 17; emph. added). Dr. Goodman once again forcefully makes this conclusive point as He alludes to the Old Testament prophet Zephaniah: "Hold thy peace at the *presence* of the Lord God, for the day of the Lord is at hand" (1:7; p. 365).

And that Day of the Lord is perhaps most famously recorded in this passage from Joel 2, with the subhead in most Bible texts, **The Terrible Visitation:**

> Blow a trumpet in Zion, and sound an alarm on My holy mountain! Let all the inhabitants of the land tremble, For the day of the LORD is coming; Surely it is near, A day of darkness and gloom, A day of clouds and thick darkness ... [When] "The sun will be turned into darkness and the moon into blood, before the great and awesome day of the Lord comes." (vv. 1-2, 2:31)

The prophet Isaiah goes into even more detail in this stunning passage:

> Behold, the day of the LORD is coming, Cruel, with fury and burning anger, To make the land a desolation; And He will exterminate its sinners from it. For the stars of heaven and their constellations will not flash forth their light; The sun will be dark when it rises, and the moon will not shed its light. Thus I will punish the world for its evil, and the wicked for their iniquity; I will also put an end to the arrogance of the proud, and abase the haughtiness of the ruthless. (13:9-11)

Then there is this, from the Gospel of Matthew, associating this event with an even more astounding Event that will become Final Culmination of Day of God:

> But immediately after the tribulation of those days the sun will be darkened, and the moon will not give its light, and the stars will fall from the sky, and the powers of the heavens will be shaken, and then the sign of the Son of Man will appear in the sky, and then all the tribes of the earth will mourn, and they will see the Son of Man coming on the clouds of the sky with power and great glory. And He will send forth His angels with a great trumpet and they will gather together His elect from the four winds, from one end of the sky to the other. (24:29-31)

And so it begins, dear friends. So it begins.

Blessed Hope in the Midst of Chaos

So here is The Day of God's Wrath unleashed for truly the first time, making the Days of Lot and Noah pale in their respective intensity. Thus my argument, that **The Sixth Seal** is the shattering of the natural order into literal and symbolic pieces, indeed, *the very End of History as we have known it,* when all with which we are familiar is brought to utter ruin.

And yet, for the peoples of God and all the peoples of the earth who read this in time, there is a providential, blazing Shaft of Light in the midst of this darkened tunnel. There shall be one group who indeed will not only be able to stand, but even to *Rise* out of this cascading blood and fire and smoke – but only one. So read on, to see and hopefully grasp hold of that Light as if your life depended on it.

Because it most assuredly does, more than you may realize.

Chapter 9: Revelation 7 - Interlude

Here we take a much needed, collective breath, as the first verse of Revelation 7 describes four angels standing at the four corners of the earth, given the divine task of "holding back" the four winds of judgment that are about to ensue throughout the earth. As Scripture tells it at this point in this Cosmic Drama:

> After this I saw four angels standing at the four corners of the earth, holding back the four winds of the earth, so that no wind should blow on the earth or on the sea or on any tree. (Rev. 7:1)

So while chapter 6 was a foretaste of God's Wrath, with many terrifying signs accompanying such dire warning, the full measure of God's Anger has not yet been spilt. For there is some preliminary work on the earth and in heaven prior to the unleashing of those Four Winds, and **One Event** in particular that must first take place, which is the heart of much current controversy.

THE RAPTURE OF THE CHURCH

I have always been captured by two Old Testament passages that remained for me largely obscure references to a supernatural event that will quite literally further shatter the foundations of human reason and the very laws of nature. They are both found in the prophecies of Isaiah, the first one embedded in an historical description of Israel's idolatry:

> The righteous man perishes, and no man takes it to heart; And devout men are taken away, while no one understands. For the righteous man is taken away from evil, He enters into peace; They rest in their beds, each one who walked in his upright way. (Isaiah 57:1-2)

Several commentaries note that this merely refers to the death of the righteous, and leave it there. But as I again drilled down on some key words, I concluded somewhat differently. The term for "taken away" for example is from the Hebrew, *acaph,* translated as: To gather, to remove, assemble or collect, receive to, or otherwise remove, importantly, "the righteous." More to the point of this thesis, it is also rendered as, *to escape or disappear* (Strong, 2016).

The second passage from Isaiah is more familiar to those of us who study eschatology. And it reinforces in a bit more detail what we find in the quotation above:

> Come, my people, enter into your rooms, and close your doors behind you; Hide for a little while, until indignation runs its course. For behold, the Lord is about to come out from His place to punish the inhabitants of the earth for their iniquity; And the earth will reveal her bloodshed and will no longer cover her slain. (Isaiah 26:20-21)

The two key terms here begin with "hide," defined by the Hebrew, *chabah*, which translates as, to secret [oneself], withdraw into privacy, conceal, or otherwise "hide from judgment" (Strong, 2016). The second term, "indignation," is defined by the Hebrew, *Za'am,* a word clearly and only used to refer to "God's fury, rage, anger, or Wrath" (capitalization used for emphasis; Zodhiates, 1990, p. 1722).

Thus both passages promote the view of God's Rescue of the Church from His Wrath in what is called **The Rapture,** and holds that believers in the Messiah will be "caught up" to be with Him in the clouds <u>prior</u> to the pouring forth of His Wrath. This view is recorded in St. Paul's First Letter to the church at Thessalonica:

> For the Lord Himself will descend from heaven with a shout [or 'cry of command'], with the voice of the archangel, and with the trumpet of God; and the dead in Christ shall rise first. Then we who are alive and remain shall be caught up together with them in the clouds to

meet the Lord in the air, and thus we shall always be with the Lord. (1 Thess. 4:16-17)

This will happen, despite many today who argue that it shall not. The only real question remaining concerns just *when* this Event takes place and not, by any theological stretch, if. However, most Traditionalists (Pre-Tribulationists) have always presumed that the Seal Judgments were the startup of that God's Wrath, and therefore the Rapture will occur before those judgments take place. We take a different view.

Throughout this book, I have argued consistently, biblically and rationally that God's people are not appointed to His Wrath, as Paul's Letter states incontrovertibly: "For God has not destined us for wrath, but for obtaining salvation through our Lord Jesus Christ" (1 Thess. 5:9). Significantly, the word for "wrath" here is from the Greek term, *Orge*, a word referring to "impulsive, violent passion; abhorrence of sin; indignation, vengeance, punishment, judgment," or by implication, Rage, as distinguished from other Greek terms used for mere anger or a lesser wrath (Zodhiates, 1990, p. 3706). The best I can describe such special, Divine Anger is that which burns white-hot in the heart of God, in response to worldwide iniquity run amok.

It is therefore the proposal of this work, along with two commentaries that came before my own, that the Rapture of the Church of Jesus Christ takes place on **The Day of the Lord,** somewhere just prior to or between the onset of God's Wrath in the Sixth Seal, and the commencing of the Trumpet Judgments following the opening of the Seventh Seal. Two variations of this idea have been presented before (Rosenthal, 1990; VanKampen, 1992), but I take the unique position that just before, perhaps only a microsecond before the appearance of the Wrath of God on the earth, indeed, "in the twinkling of an eye" (1 Cor. 15:52), He literally, visibly, and some would say, *catastrophically* rescues all followers of Christ in a massive upsweep into the clouds that leaves the rapidly disintegrating world order behind.

The reason I say, "catastrophically," is due to the Greek word used for this Catching Away in the passage cited previously from Paul's First Letter to the Thessalonians. The word used there is, *harpazo*, meaning "to seize or carry away suddenly *by force*" (4:17; Zodhiates, 1990, p. 2112, emph. added). I recall many years ago a lovely, elderly lady named Grace came to me to share three dreams she had of this Event, and described it as something akin to a jet plane flying low above the ground, in the wake of which was a vacuum of indescribable power that swept up all in its wake.

In some visual support of what Ms. Grace and the passage she shared with me decades ago, was something I noticed recently at a viewing of the only slightly attended film, Risen, starring Ralph Fiennes as a Roman tribune in search of the truth of those turbulent times. Times, significantly, not unlike our own. While I found the movie's acting, film score and overall production qualities both superb and engaging, it was the end of the story that captured my biblical imagination concerning the Rapture Event. As the disciples were gathered to receive the Lord's final instructions and bid farewell to the Messiah at the Mount of Olives near Bethany, a heretofore unprecedented and stupendous thing happened. They are nearly blown back by the sheer force of the Ascension.

Let's visit the full text to see what occurred:

> Now when He had spoken these things, while they watched, **He was taken up**, and a cloud received Him out of their sight. And while they looked steadfastly toward heaven as He went up, behold, two men stood by them in white apparel, who also said, "Men of Galilee, why do you stand gazing up into heaven? This same Jesus, who was taken up from you into heaven, will so come in like manner as you saw Him go into heaven." (Acts 1:9-11 NKJV; emph. added)

Now notice the phrase, "He was taken up." The Greek terms used here is *epairo,* translated literally as "exalted by being hoisted up." Drilling down a bit more, "hoisted" is from a Dutch root word for being "drawn up with ropes and pulleys." Which in turn strongly implies *a raising by force.* The idea here is that for Christ (or anyone) to be likewise "lifted up" in defiance of the known laws of physics, *great power* is needed. Thus does the film depict the Lord's Ascension as a powerful and breathtaking Event, in keeping with my sense of what the Rapture must require for us all to be likewise taken up. I therefore highly recommend your seeing this film, if only for this one important lesson concerning our Promise of being raised up, *just like Him.* Selah.

While hardly a scientific explanation of something so unprecedented in human experience, I remain impressed by the supernatural "Force" indeed that will be required for this to happen, clearly implicit in the language chosen by the Holy Spirit to describe such an extraordinary event. This, not unlike the very indescribable *Power* that raised Christ from the dead, which some scientists have likened unto a controlled, thermonuclear event (e.g., Skurka, 2014).

And all of this, **on the very same Day** -- the nearly violent exodus of hundreds of millions from the earth, while the very Cosmos is being shaken quite literally to its limits. Terror, tumult and chaos beyond human description indeed, for all those who *remain.* And as Hill and McMahon point out in their online commentary concerning the reasoning for such a claim: "This truth causes us to make a strong distinction between Israel and the church which is His body. Israel was identified as the people of the tribulation by Daniel [9:24-27]" (n.d.).

To sum up: The Church is Raptured, having spent their times in relative difficulty, deprivation and danger; then the Jews are appointed to *their* Day of Troubles about to come. Scripture teaches, however, that after this Time of Jacob's Distress, "all Israel shall be saved" (Rom. 11:26).

The Sealing of the 144,000

In strong support of this view, there is in Chapter 7 an unmistakable reference to God's protections over a certain group that remains after the Rapture has taken place. While believing Christians are evacuated from the earth due to their sincere obedience, as with the Church at Philadelphia, the Scripture further clarifies this concerning The Rapture:

> I know your deeds. Behold, I have put before you an open door which no one can shut, because you have a little power, and have kept My word, and have not denied My name ... Because you have kept the word of My perseverance, I also will keep you from the hour of testing, that hour which is about to come upon the whole world, to test those who dwell upon the earth. (Rev. 3:8, 10; emph. added)

The context, language and symmetry with both Old and New Testament doctrine are again unmistakable here: True Christians do not remain to endure the Great Tribulation which follows the Sixth Seal. Because they have persevered to the end (Mt. 24:13), they are literally "kept" from [*tereo ek* in the Greek- "I will keep you out of"] that hour of testing, via the Rapture of His own. Therefore, beloved of the Lord, be greatly comforted by this (1 Thess. 4:18).

Thus in the wake of our catastrophic absence, God institutes the next phase of the great End Time Plan for the earth with the setting apart of a very special group of New Evangelists. While arguments still persist over the identity of this group, a literal reading of this section – clearly the proper hermeneutic here – shows that they are Jews, specially selected for ministry in the midst of the fiery Tribulation about to follow.

> [And an angel cried out with a loud voice], "Do not harm the earth or the sea or the trees until we have sealed the bond-servants of our God on their foreheads." And I

heard the number of those who were sealed, one hundred and forty-four thousand sealed from every tribe of the sons of Israel ... (Rev. 7:3-4)

Notice that these Jews are "sealed" from all harm that will follow, or literally stamped (*sphragizo*) for security and divine preservation (Zodhiates, 1990, p. 2287). This so that they shall go out into the mayhem fully protected and enabled to supernaturally proclaim God's Message of Truth, Love, and great Power during the dark and fiery times to follow.

Age of the Gentiles to the Age of the Jews

Theologian, lawyer, and Rhodes Scholar Earl Thames offers what I consider clarity of reasoning for this grand strategy:

But before the unleashing of God's wrath the angels are told to "hold back", and there is the sealing of the 144,000 of the tribes of Israel, and the vision of the total company of the redeemed, "a multitude which no man can number," around the throne in Heaven [Rev. 7:9; in contrast to those in Rev. 20:4]. This would seem to indicate that the earth has been reaped, the Harvest has been completely gathered in. If this is so, then the opening of the Seventh Seal and the terrible events which follow, take place *after* Christians have been removed from the earth. (2014, p. 65; emph. added)

So it is that we enter upon this **Cosmic Interlude,** while the 144,000 Jews are sealed in order to "take over" from the Church, the divine charge to spread the Gospel during the Great Tribulation, since Christians are no longer on the earth, having fulfilled both their Cultural Commission and the Great Commission (cf. Mt. 5:13-16, 28:29-30).

First to the Jews and then to the Gentiles, and now indeed, fully and finally back to the Jews. William McDonald's superb commentary (1995) wonderfully summarizes this phase of transfer, if you will, from one people of God to the next:

> The 144,000 are clearly Jewish believers, not members of some 20th century Gentile cult. These Jewish saints are saved during the early part of the Tribulation. The seal on their foreheads brands them as belonging to God and guarantees that they will be *preserved alive* during the ensuing seven years. (p. 2363; emph. added)

And so we move to the Final Phase of this epochal transformation from one Age (of the Gentiles) to the prophesied Time of Jacob's Distress (Jer. 30:7), where Israel shall all the more become the *Epicenter* of God's attentions, as Joel Rosenberg prefers to call this unique place on the earth (2006).

Chapter 10: The Seventh Seal Judgment

As we come out of the time of sealing of the 144,000 Jews for their Tribulation mission for God, a most curious and inarguably unique moment in the Universe takes place. The Apostle John records it thus: "When the Lamb broke the seventh seal, there was **silence in heaven** for about half an hour" (Rev. 8:1; emph. added). Two key elements stand out here, the first of which is this stunning Silence in Heaven, by which we can take to mean throughout the entire cosmic order. As MacDonald (1995) reverently observes:

> After the parenthesis of chapter 7 ... we now come to the seventh and final seal. This is introduced by a thirty minute silence in heaven, *an awesome hush* which precedes ever-deepening judgments. (p. 2365; emph. added)

Why a half an hour? While again I cannot teach this as canon, I remind of the idea captured in the title of a book titled, God Counts by W. E. Filmer (2011). In that work, he proposes that the number 30 signifies the Blood of Christ, dedication, and maturity. Thus by this interpretation, the Universe and Mankind have come full course, and are now set for God's Judgments.

TRUMPETS

In verse two of the eighth chapter, John describes the following: "And I saw the seven angels who stand before God; and *seven trumpets* were given to them" (emph. added). Thames (2014) this time recounts the raw power of this moment in time, as he introduces what will follow this Silence in Heaven:

> Trumpets are the events of the Seventh seal, then the silence signified the awesomeness of the moment of judgment – *the Universe was still*. It was a very solemn

moment. It should be noted that the events about to be related are those about which all men have been warned. The events about to be related are those from which Christ has saved His people. (p. 66; emph. added)

It is almost as if the entire Cosmic Order bends and bows, as in a mournful, dreadful prayer for those about to experience what is come to them. By the reasoning presented previously, we may also presume that The Church is now in Heaven, in sacred Silence as well. And all recognize God's Heart is always that none, none should perish but that all would come to Him and find real Life (2 Pet. 3:9).

But He has waited long enough and cannot delay any longer.

So as I draw this study to a close, I depart somewhat from the scholarly literature and venture into the realm of the inexplicable. As I mentioned in the opening chapters, there have been many reports over the past ten years, beginning after the horrific events of September 11, 2001, of **trumpet sounds** in the heavens. They are easily located on YouTube, and sound very much like an eerie, mammoth Shofar emplaced high up in the sky, or ram's horn that the Hebrews used in ancient times to signal some special event. Of particular importance to this study's consideration of Trumpets, is what the Jews call *Teshuvah*, or the word tightly woven into the fabric of the High Holy Days, which call us to Repentance.

So do I propose that these celestial trumpet blasts, these eschatological Shofar Alarms are very possibly *God's Final Call to Repentance*, before His Holy Wrath falls upon the whole earth and all the nations. While many will come to know God during the Great Tribulation about to commence, it will be at a great price indeed (Rev. 20: 4). Thus better to come even now, right now. For as Hebrew tradition notes, these days of Teshuvah are rightly known as *The Days of Awe,* and are designed to provide everyone with the opportunity to survey the condition of their lives and hearts and get right with God. Selah.

GOD'S FULL WRATH

Following the Great Silence of half an hour then, there is described another mystical occurrence in which, as MacDonald writes, "The prayers of all the saints ascend to the Father through Him [Jesus, who] ... takes much incense to offer it with the prayers. The incense speaks of the fragrance of His Person and work" (1995, p. 2365; Rev. 8:3-4). This is quickly followed by peals of thunder and lightning and an earthquake, as the angel of the Lord casts the censer in which all this was contained to the earth (v. 5). Thus it is that the prayers of the saints at this time return to the earth as Wrath is about to spill upon all the nations. And then that Wrath ever more fully and terribly cascades in rapid succession as the **Trumpet Judgments** commence.

The First Trumpet: Hail and fire mixed with blood which burns up a third of the earth and trees, and all the green grass (v. 7).

The Second Trumpet: A great mountain (likely a giant comet) burning with fire crashes into the sea, rendering a third of it dead as filled with blood along with a third of all sea creatures and ships utterly destroyed (v. 8).

The Third Trumpet: Another "great star" (comet) fell from the skies, burning like a torch Scripture says, falling on a third of all the rivers and springs of waters, the name of which is Wormwood from which many men die because the waters were so bitter [Note: Russian word for Wormwood is Chernobyl] (v. 10).

The Fourth Trumpet: A third of the sun and moon and stars were struck, so that a third of their light was snuffed out, and an eagle soars above saying with a loud voice, "Woe, woe, woe, to those who dwell on the earth, because of the remaining blasts of the trumpet of the three angels who are about to sound!" (v. 12-13).

At this point the world descends into those *Final Three Trumpet Judgments,* as horrific as they are, to be followed by an even more severe sequence of calamities in the form of **Bowl or Vial Judgments** (Chs. 9-16), the breadth, depth and enormity of which reach far beyond the bounds and purposes of this small book. Thus do I commend to the reader to read, as a favorite broadcast journalist used to say, "the rest of the story," for themselves if any of this has prodded your interest (Paul Harvey, 1984).

More importantly, I call each of you to carefully consider a question first posed by the brilliant Christian philosopher, Francis Schaeffer in his 1976 book: *How Should We Then Live?* I first read this book as a new follower of The Messiah in the early 1980s, when the world was in a seemingly much better place. Today, of course, the world is very different indeed, requiring each of us to bend toward Teshuvah all the more, as America and all the nations appear to be more and more, Slouching Toward Gomorrah, as Robert H. Bork put it in 1996.

But the good news is and ever shall be beautifully captured in the now classic piece by Irish poet William B. Yeats in a work titled, "The Second Coming":

> Turning and turning in the widening gyre
> The falcon cannot hear the falconer;
> Things fall apart; the centre cannot hold;
> Mere anarchy is loosed upon the world,
> The blood-dimmed tide is loosed, and everywhere
> The ceremony of innocence is drowned;
> The best lack all conviction, while the worst
> Are full of passionate intensity.
> Surely some revelation is at hand;
> Surely the Second Coming is at hand.
> The Second Coming! Hardly are those words out
> When a vast image out of Spiritus Mundi

Troubles my sight: somewhere in sands of the desert
A shape with lion body and the head of a man,
A gaze blank and pitiless as the sun,
Is moving its slow thighs, while all about it
Reel shadows of the indignant desert birds.
The darkness drops again; but now I know
That twenty centuries of stony sleep
Were vexed to nightmare by a rocking cradle,
And what rough beast, its hour come round at last,
Slouches towards Bethlehem to be born? (1920)

And all of God's people, and all those who now vow to seek Him perhaps as never before, while there is still a little time, together say with the Apostle John at Patmos so very long ago: "Amen. Come Lord Jesus." For He is coming, and coming very quickly! (Rev. 22:20-21)

Epilogue: How Shall We Then Live?

So what now? If as I have proposed, the End Times have already begun to envelop all the peoples of the earth, and are very likely to intensify in the months and years just ahead, what then are we to do? What should be our reasonable course in such an Era, this period just before Messiah is about to Return when His fiercest Judgments are about to be visited upon all Mankind? Or again as Dr. Schaeffer brilliantly posed the question so perfectly long ago: *How Should We Then Live*, beloved? How shall we plan for and live out these Days of Expectation in a way that honors God, protects our family and helps our neighbor? (Mt. 23:37-40).

To address that important question, I propose **Three Basic Strategies** for survival and success in the potentially difficult days ahead of us: Spiritual Preparation; Financial Preparation; and Physical Preparation. And if you think this all hyperbolic hand wringing or irrational alarmism, recall to mind *Pascal's Wager* applied to our times. In its diluted form, it runs something like this: Pascal's argument is that it is in one's own best interest to behave as if God exists and His Words be true, since the possibility of eternal punishment in Hell outweighs any advantage of believing otherwise. You lose nothing by believing, but you lose catastrophically all if you choose to disbelieve (Pensées, part III, §233, c. 1650). Applied here, if God's Words on Last Things be indeed true and accurately understood, then it is eminently reasonable to take precautions as potential or probable danger approaches. To do otherwise becomes the ultimate Fool's Errand.

So to work.

SPIRITUAL PREPARATION

A pastor friend of mine from years back once taught me something that stayed with me all these years concerning the work of the Holy Spirit of God. Roughly paraphrased, he surmised: "God's Spirit doesn't just work on the hearts of believers, but on each individual based on where he or she is along his or her search for Truth and God." I believe this is biblically accurate, and that it brings hope and promise to us all, the saved and unsaved alike. And here's why. The Prophet Joel, quoted by the Apostle Paul, taught us that this would happen in the Last Days:

> And it will come about after this that I will pour out My Spirit *on all mankind* ... And it will come about that whoever calls on the name of the Lord will be delivered. (Joel 2:28, 32; emph. added)

Notice that word, "all." It means all, never mind the theological debates which rage to the contrary. God's heart is that, again, *all* should have every opportunity to be saved from the trials yet to come, and that none would perish but come to repent and ask God to take over the life of the seeker (2 Pet. 3:9). Thus He meets every single man, woman and child right where they are, most especially when they cry out for Him, no matter their spiritual or theological state.

So the first thing to do to prepare for the rough times ahead is to quite simply, **Get right with God.** This doesn't boil down to a set formula or particular prayer as much as to a heartfelt plea for God to indeed, take control of one's life and all its mayhem and mistakes, which is for all intents and purposes and in varying degrees, reeling out of control. As I alluded to in the Foreward, I did this on October 30, 1979, just one day before I had planned to take my own life on Halloween the very next day. While many things didn't improve right away, there was this inexorable pull toward God's Peace and a meaningful Life that is undeniable, as I look back over the years, now more than 35 year later at the age of 72 as I write these words. So yes, just ask Him to *take over* as a first step toward being rebirthed into extraordinary Love, Truth and Power that are accessible in no other way (Jn. 3:16; Rom. 10:9-10). And all the rest shall surely follow.

Second, then start the earnest work of *renewing your mind* in two distinct stages, as we recall again that as a man or woman thinks, so they speak, act and become (Prov. 23:7a; Rom. 12:1-2). This of course begins first by reading the Bible, starting with the Book of Genesis, then to the Psalms and Proverbs, and finally to the Gospel of John through to the end. This is important to a much needed shift of perspective in one's way of life that we don't humanly have the power to change. But as we learn more of Him and His View of things, asking His Spirit for all the power and wisdom He will make available to us, we will become more and more transformed into the very Likeness of Him. The likes of which I can personally testify is a stupendous thing to experience (cf. Acts 1:8; Eph. 5:18; Bennett, 1994).

This second stage involves also studying biblical literature written by mature men and women of God in various books, journal articles and even online blogs which reflect their best effort in what I earlier called a richly biblical worldview (See Sources & Notes section). One of the best proponents of this important phase of growth in God is the Oxford trained student of C. S. Lewis, Harry Blamires, who wrote The Christian Mind (1963) to address the question: How Should a Christian Think?

Even back then, Blamires lamented the fact that Christians had withdrawn their "Christian consciousness from the fields of public, commercial, and social life," to the disastrous consequence of losing the entire culture (1963, p. 27). Thus he addressed The Marks of the Christian Mind viz. the crucial importance of acquiring a supernatural orientation to such things as the nature of evil, the conception of truth, acceptance of proper authority, concern for the person, and taking on what he called "a sacramental cast," involving the ability to live a life in rich appreciation of hope, love, truth, and beauty, even in the midst of great difficulty (Part 2, & p. 173).

For those more advanced in the Christian faith, there comes still another phase involving the very necessary spiritual skill associated with *spiritual warfare*. Certainly in times of Satanic activity through the various Seal Judgments involving his wrath, there will be the need to combat his forces with those of Heaven, largely through aggressive, authoritative intercessory prayer. Christ's reminder to His disciples that we have such authority is crystal clear: "Behold, I have given you authority to tread on serpents and scorpions, and over all the power of the enemy, and nothing will injure you" (Luke 10:19).

For additional information on this important spiritual charge, consult Paul Thigpen's, Manual for Spiritual Warfare (2014), and two engaging earlier novels dealing with spiritual warfare: Frank Peretti's, This Present Darkness (1986) and J. Parker Hudson's grittier work On the Edge (1994). More recently there is a fascinating book by Neill G. Russell, Newton's Riddle (2015), that dramatizes Isaac Newton's nearly life-long search for the Times of the Second Advent of Christ. And of course there is the delightful movie, War Room (Kendrick, 2015) starring Karen Abercrombie as Miss Clara Williams, whose award-winning performance about how to wage sustained militant prayer provides sound and brilliant counsel for such activity.

Finally, it is also of utmost importance that a follower of Christ *share God with others* through that prayerful, biblically-informed worldview with all who are willing to hear it. This is to be enacted in two ways, primarily, both of which I wrote about earlier. One, fulfill the Great Commission by sharing the Gospel message when prompted by the Holy Spirit to do so, leading others to His New Life, especially when they are in dire circumstances and are hungry to hear about Him. And second, fulfill the Cultural Commission by staying active in community activities such as school board meetings, local political groups which espouse biblically conservative policies regarding such hot button issues as abortion, Jewish Israel, sexuality issues, and any other way to be a servant to your community. In sum, be salt and light to this present darkness in every way possible.

FINANCIAL PREPARATION

Now here I must defer to vastly wiser thinkers and writers than myself, since frankly I still struggle to even balance my checkbook each month. But the rules for **managing our money** in dark times are rather simple, and grounded not only in Scripture but also in plain old, homespun common sense. So in light of the growing probability of economic chaos coming soon, we ought to take just a few practical steps that most experts tell us would be wise to consider, so here are just a few.

Recent developments in the banking industry here and overseas ought to give us serious pause regarding our financial standing. An alarming report published in several venues was titled, "The IMF Proposes Global Wealth Confiscation," detailing world banks' readiness to actually begin to tax private accounts in order to sustain and balance their own, massively over-invested accounts. Second, various reports of banks beginning to more severely limit the amount and frequency of ATM withdrawals suggests that the banks are indeed in deep waters (cf. Ernst, 2016).

In light of these developments and other events described in the Third Seal chapter – and supposing that the banks begin to fail or at least increasingly restrict our access to our own accounts, as we saw take place in both Greece and China recently – I would strongly suggest you follow my attorney's counsel a few years back to avoid placing most of your money in your local bank. Rather, it may well be much safer to *purchase a strong box* to keep a sizable sum of cash there (ideally, about $1,000), rather than rely on the vicissitudes of world markets which interact, sometimes disastrously, with our banks. In that same regard, we are investing a modest amount in precious metals, especially silver, which remains easily affordable at least for now, and avoiding like the plague the stock market highs and lows which we witness taking place on a daily basis.

Second, *downsizing* is almost always a good idea, though in these times may soon become absolutely necessary. Reassess your lifestyle and start to put away (sell or donate or both) various excessive material things, toys that we no longer use or need, and yes, that massive house you barely qualified for that is half empty since the kids left for college. And speaking of college, don't do what we did and leverage yourself into an economic box canyon with hundreds of thousands of dollars of student loan debt. And if you have not done so already, establish a manageable payback strategy that moves you toward payoff as soon as is practical.

For more details on getting debt free, or at least debt-lowered, consult such wizards as Dave Ramsey (2009) and his excellent recommendations for a Total Money Makeover. The point in all of this is to throw off all excess financial baggage that would weigh you down in drastic economic times. This to be able to, if called upon, move at the relative drop of a hat should the Lord provide a different calling, job or location for the family that may be more suitable and reliable in difficult times. In sum, live light, travel light, and most importantly, think Light in the times to come, for the good of all.

PHYSICAL PREPARATION

Here I don't wish to appear as some rank survivalist (or "prepper") necessarily, hunkering down for doomsday and living 50 feet underground. Rather, I propose what I believe the Lord instructed me to follow as a **Thirty Day Plan**. Thus there are just a few rudimentary things we can easily and inexpensively do to prepare for a time when we may be required to live off the grid for about a month or so. No, don't move to a farm in Montana and start raising veggies and sheep quite yet, while training to become an expert huntsman, though on reflection, perhaps that wouldn't be so bad. Instead, follow some very simple, common sense rules for surviving on your own for a short period of time.

One, barring religious reasons for not doing so, purchase at least one firearm and a sufficient supply of ammunition to last for about a month. This, to be blunt, while you still can. I won't take the time here to document the many governmental assaults on both the First and Second Amendments, but clearly only a hermit would deny the fact that Americans are fast losing ground on our Constitutional freedoms, most rapidly and importantly, the first two.

Second, also seriously consider buying a small, gas-powered generator suitable to the size of your dwelling, with enough gasoline to last for about a month. And for those who already have a gas grill, purchase extra canisters of butane for that same period of time. The obvious point here is to be able to generate heat and light for both comfort and cooking sufficiently stored foodstuffs during times when the weather or power loss demand it. Also think about other power needs such as flashlights with long-life batteries, candles, matches, and a short wave radio for listening in on any emergency broadcasts during a time when normal television and radio signals are lost.

Finally, some sort of water purifier will become a must if the city or country loses power, since our water supplies are driven by electricity. Stocking up on bottled water is of course a good idea, but there may come a time when we will have to foray for our own water wherever it may be found, and a purifier would become a necessity in such circumstances. A long list of such devices that would be used for camping and backpacking are easily accessible online for relatively low cost.

In sum, pastor and author Carl Gallups has just released a book that describes in much more detail the spiritual and practical advice given here. The title says a lot: Be Thou Prepared: Equipping the Church for Persecution and Times of Trouble (2015). I believe he captures both the spirit of the times and offers wise, realistic counsel to us all for what lies ahead. And that is what this closing section has attempted to do as well.

Last Thoughts

In all of this of course, there are multiple publications and blogs that can better prepare us for dire situations, but all I have done here again is to list the minimal, practical things to do in order to *be ready*, should the times require us to do just that. But I must quickly reiterate that the First Step in this section, **becoming spiritually prepared,** dramatically mitigates all the rest that we can do to weather the storms ahead. I cannot emphasize enough the importance of having God's Cover during these times. That includes *believers* who need to get their lifestyle choices in better order, and for the *unbeliever* to commit to Christ in a simple, sincere prayer of dedication to His service.

Which reminds of that Old Testament passage cited earlier, that is fitting to this entire message as we conclude.

> Come, my people, enter into your rooms, and close your doors behind you; Hide for a little while, until indignation [or rage] runs its course. For behold, the Lord is about to come out from His place to punish the inhabitants of the earth for their iniquity; And the earth will reveal her bloodshed, and will no longer cover her slain. (Isaiah 26:20-21)

Thus do we have a final illustration of a fully eschatological *Mysterium Tremendum* of an altogether different order, a Divine Promise if you will, of a Hiding Place for all the saints during this unprecedented time of fiery Indignation and global Chaos.

This last reflection therefore brings us to a question that is on the mind of most thoughtful Americans in these Last Days, one dramatically reflected in the drafting of this book: **Can the nation be saved?** That is, can we retrieve it from

133

this seemingly inexorable slide toward historic oblivion, or is it too late? Until the very early morning sometime in September, 2015, I thought the worst. But having just attended a men's breakfast to listen to the vision of a Denver-based speaker named Herb Reese, I was moved toward a ray of hope for us who continue to labor for renewal in these dark times.

Mr. Reese passionately argued that if a nation desires to "get back" to firm footing, it need only heed a single ancient prophecy from Isaiah, still again: "Learn to do good; Seek justice, Reprove the ruthless; Defend the orphan, Plead for the widow" (1:17). So rather than run the commentaries or do another word study, let me quote richly from Scott Tibbs, a conservative online blogger who has a heart for what Reese envisions and also strikes a powerful balance between a Christian's call to compassion for the sinner on the one hand, and the more activist, even militant, charge to rescue the weak and innocent on the other. Think abortion here. Think sex abuse and the trafficking of little children here. In sum: *Think rescue here.*

> Someone who has truly repented of his sins and seeks to be redeemed by the blood of Jesus Christ will be forgiven for his sins, no matter how evil and perverse those sins might be. From the person who steals a small item from the supermarket to the worst Nazi war criminal, there is no sinner so depraved that the blood of Jesus Christ cannot redeem that person from his sins. But that unbelievably merciful reassurance does not and should never be used to deny the earthly consequences for sin, especially horrible brutality committed against innocent people. The state is called to bear the sword against these people, and Christians are called to speak God's truth about how God hates the oppression of the innocent. (ConservaTibbs.com, October 7, 2009)

This in furious rejection of a passive, even cowardly and nearly criminal indifference to the plight of those who suffer grievously under our watch.

And one final note on the importance of the political nation that is in such chaos these days across the entire ideological spectrum, from far Left to Center to far Right. While I would never propose that politics is *the* answer, I wholeheartedly believe that it is undeniably part of it. Here's why. My strong recommendation here is built on the premise that America has declined catastrophically in direct proportion to her rejection of the God of her Founding. Thus it is my considered view that we must elect conservative, morally principled leaders of strong, biblically defined **character** who can (a) seek God's wisdom and courage on a regular basis, and (b) thus govern steadily in times of tumult and disorder.

Conservative journalist Steve McCann, writing again for my favorite American Thinker journal, says this in his intense comparison of Donald Trump and Ted Cruz in an article with a telling title, "The Closet Statist and the Constitutional Conservative":

> Ted Cruz by temperament, experience and accomplishments is well qualified to be the next president. *This nation is at the point of no return* and in order to avoid the abyss over the horizon it must reverse course by returning to the basis of its founding: Individual liberty, opportunity and limited government as expounded in the Constitution. Ted Cruz, as Rush Limbaugh has pointed out, is the closest candidate to Ronald Reagan we will see in our lifetime and in my opinion the best candidate to oversee this course correction. (2016; emph. added)

Thus I believe that if we do not or cannot elect someone like Senator Cruz, steeped since childhood in Biblical and Constitutional wisdom with great political skill, I do not believe that the Republic will frankly be able to weather another four to eight years like the last eight under President Obama's wholesale rejection of the Jewish-Christian God in clear favor of the Islamic god. It remains to be seen if President Donald Trump can prove these principles to be ignored and still yield a cultural reformation.

So yes, *if* the Church will lead in such things, and encourage political leaders to follow suit, then and only then will it be possible for America to return to her former glory as a light to the nations. But it would take an act of God Himself to fuel such a massive change of hearts in this direction, especially among our pastors and church leaders who are already burdened with much and likely quite weary from it all (Smith, 2014).

And yet, and yet, our leaders must once again take on the cloaks of the Black Robed Regiment of old, and simply, lovingly throw down the gauntlet in the pursuit of both the Great Commission and Cultural Commission, to fight till their last breath to bring salvation, yes, but also rescue and healing to the most hurting among us. Lest indeed we lose the nation fully. **Time is very short indeed,** so we must all act, and act now, in concert with Biblical teachings and sound, canny and courageous leadership in a world gone nearly, fully rogue.

One final observation. In a blog that I write for my Facebook account, I recently took serious stock of the upcoming presidential election on Tuesday, November 8, 2016. After considerable prayer and intense study of both the Scriptures and hundreds of articles, journals and other political analysis, I came to the conclusion that this election was *A Referendum* of sorts for the people of the United States of America. In comparing the days of Sodom with those of today's world and nation, I proposed this in a column entitled, "On America in the Crosshairs: Judgment or Mercy?":

> It is my studied view that this presidential election represents our Moment of Decision, a great Referendum

if you will, on what sort of "city' we desire. And if I am correct in this assessment, the question fairly burns: Will enough Americans do the right thing? No matter which candidate you support (my own choice is crystal clear), we must drill down and ask ourselves to discern, to the best of our intellectual and spiritual ability, which candidate best agrees with what Scripture would call a strong and virtuous leader. (Kelly, 2016)

I am increasingly convinced that if we don't get this election right, we will suffer the consequences of a God who may well have run out of patience with our multitude of sins and countless institutional rejections of His Most High and His Ways. In sum: We must choose well this time, since I am not at all confident that the Republic can endure still another failed presidency.

Thus in closing are we drawn down to a classic, historic and unprecedented **Crossroads:** The one branching to the Left taking us toward that gaping Abyss described again by Himmelfarb (1994) and so very many others over the years; the other to the Right, however, moving us toward what I'd call *A Grand Refreshment*, a turning toward the God who founded us at the very first. So do the Words of Moses present Americans with an Epic Choice in this day as it was with the Hebrews more than 3,400 years ago:

> I call heaven and earth to witness against you today, that I have set before you life and death, the blessing and the curse. *So choose life* in order that you may live, you and your descendants, by loving the Lord your God, by obeying His voice, and by holding fast to Him; for this is your life and the length of your days, that you may live in the land which the Lord swore to your fathers, to Abraham, Isaac, and Jacob, to give them. (Deut. 30:19-20; emph. added)

And He who sits on the Throne of God in Heaven says in thunderous refrain,

> "Behold, I am making all things new." And He said, "Write, for these words are faithful and true" ... [Then the Lamb spoke], "And behold, I am coming quickly. Blessed is he who heeds the words of the prophecy of this book" ... He who testifies to these things says, "Yes, I am coming quickly." Amen. Come, Lord Jesus! The grace of the Lord Jesus be with all. Amen. (Rev. 21:5, 22:7, 22:20-21)

So to the God of All Things be the Kingdom, and the Glory, and the Power, and the immense Wonder of it, both now and soon and very soon, and then forever and forever and forever.

Amen. For Him. DK

SOURCES & NOTES

Chapter 1

Barna, G. (2003, Dec. 3). "A Biblical Worldview Has a Radical Effect on a Person's Life." Barna.org.

Bennett, William (1999). *The Death of Outrage: Bill Clinton and the Assault on American Ideals*. New York, NY: Free Press of Glencoe.

Cicero, Marcus T. (1892). *Orations*.

Colson, Charles W. & Vaughn, Ellen Santelli (1989). *Against the Night: Living in the New Dark Ages*. Ventura, CA: Vine Books.

Creech, M. H. (2013, May 1). "Understanding The Church's Cultural Mandate and the Great Commission," *Christian Post*.

de Tocqueville, Alexis (1835). *Democracy in America: Historical-Critical Edition, 4 vols*. Indianapolis, IN: Liberty Fund.

Dobson, James (2016, June 25). "What James Dobson said in 1998 About Moral Character and the Presidency." *The Way of Improvement Leads Home*. (John Fea).

Henley, Kari (2011, Nov. 17). "Are You Obsessed With Being Busy?" *Huffington Post Healthy Living*.

Himmelfarb, Gertrude (1994). *On Looking Into the Abyss: Untimely Thoughts on Culture and Society*. New York, NY: Vintage Books.

Hunter, James Davison (1991). *Culture Wars: The Struggle To Control The Family, Art, Education, Law, And Politics In America*. New York, NY: Basic Books.

Huntington, Samuel P. (1996). *The Clash of Civilizations and the Remaking of World Order*. New York, NY: Simon & Schuster.

Jeffress, Robert (2015). *Countdown to the Apocalypse: Why ISIS and Ebola Are Only the Beginning*. Nashville, TN: Faith Words Publishers.

Johnson, Paul (1983). *Modern Times: A History of the World from the 1920s to the 1980s*. New York, NY: Harper & Row.

Onenewsnow.com.

Postman, Neil (1985). *Amusing Ourselves to Death: Public Discourse in the Age of Show Business*. New York, NY: Penguin Books.

Strong, James (2009). *Strong's Exhaustive Concordance of the Bible* (Online ed.). Peabody, MA: Hendrickson Publishers, Inc.

Veith, Jr., Gene E. (1994). *Postmodern Times: A Christian Guide to Contemporary Thought and Culture*. Wheaton, IL: Crossway Books.

Webster, Noah (1967, 1828). *American Dictionary of the English Language* (1828 Facsimile Ed.). Chesapeake, VA: Foundation for American Christian Education.

Wilkerson, David (1998). *America's Last Call*. New Kensington, PA: Whitaker House Publishers.

Woodward, Chris (2014, Aug. 1). "Barna: Many Pastors Wary of Raising 'Controversy.'"

Zacharias, Ravi (1998). *Deliver Us From Evil: Restoring the Soul in a Disintegrating Culture*. Nashville, TN: Harper Collins.

Zodhiates, Spiros (Ed.) (1990, 2008). *Hebrew-Greek Key Word Study Bible*. NASB. Chattanooga, TN: AMG Publishers.

Chapter 2

Easley, Kendall H. & Max Anders (1999). *Holman New Testament Commentary – Revelation*. Nashville, TN: Holman Bible Publishers.

Barclay, William (1959). *The Revelation of John*. Edinburgh, Scotland: The Saint Andrew Press.

Buchanan, Pat J. (2015, Aug. 24). "Is Trumpism," *WND*.

"Dominionism" (2015, Sept. 24). *Wikipedia*.

House, H. Wayne & Ice, Thomas (1988). *Dominion Theology: Blessing or Curse? An Analysis of Christian Reconstructionism*. Portland, OR: Multnomah Publishing.

Ladd, George E. (1972). *A Commentary on the Revelation of John*. Grand Rapids, MI: William B. Eerdmans Publishing.

Montgomery, John W. (1986). *History and Christianity*. Bloomington, MN: Bethany House Publishing.

Prasch, J. J. (2014). *Harpazo: The Intra-Seal Rapture of the Church*. Trafalgar, Vic Australia: Moriel Ministries.

Rogers, Jay (2008, April). "The Postmillenial View," *The Forerunner*.

Chapter 3

Balogh, Kim (2013, Aug. 16). "The Love Gospel," *Christian Watchman*.

Colson, Charles (1999). *How Now Shall We Live?* Carol Stream, IL: Tyndale House Publishers.

Delia, J., O'Keefe, B. J., & O'Keefe, D. J. (1982). The Constructivist Approach to communication. In F. E. X. Dance (Ed.), *Human Communication Theory: Comparative Essays*, 147-191. New York: Harper and Row.

Gregg, Steve (1997). *Revelation: Four Views: A Parallel Commentary*. Nashville, TN: Thomas Nelson Publishers.

Hendley, Jesse M. (1985). *Fifth Horseman of the Apocalypse*. Grand Rapids, MI: Kregel Publications.

Leclaire, Jennifer (2014, Aug. 13). "Most Pastors Avoid Controversial Issues," *Charisma News*.

Montaigne, David (2014). *Antichrist 2016-2019: Mystery Babylon, Barack Obama & the Islamic Caliphate*. Seattle, WA: Amazon Digital Services.

Montgomery, Ted (2008). "Parallels Between the Six Seals and the Olivet Discourse." Tedmontgomery.com.

Morris, Henry M. (1983). *The Revelation Record: A Scientific and Devotional Commentary on the Prophetic Book of the End of Times.* Grand Rapids, MI: Eerdmans Publishing.

Nash, Ronald (1992). *Worldviews in Conflict: Choosing Christianity in a World of Ideas.* Grand Rapids, MI: Zondervan Publishers.

Naugle, David (2002). *Worldview: History of a Concept.* Grand Rapids, MI: Eerdmans Publishing.

Noebel, David (1994). *Understanding the Times.* Carson, CA: Harvest Press.

"None's on the Rise" (2012, Oct. 9). Washington, DC: Pew Research Center.

Richardson, Joel (2006). *Antichrist: Islam's Awaited Messiah.* Enumclaw, WA: Winepress Publishers.

Rosenberg, Joel (2006). *Epicenter: Why Current Rumblings in the Middle East Will Change Your Future.* Carol Stream, IL: Tyndale House Publishers.

Schaeffer, Francis (1976). *How Should We Then Live: The Rise and Decline of Western Thought and Culture.* Wheaton, IL: Crossway Books.

Schaeffer, Francis (1984). *The Great Evangelical Disaster.* Wheaton, IL: Crossway Books.

Sire, James W. (2009). *The Universe Next Door: A Basic Worldview Catalog.* Downers Grove, IL: InterVarsity Press.

Stice, Ralph W. (2005). *From 9/11 to 666 : The Convergence of Current Events, Biblical Prophecy and the Vision of Islam.* Ozark, AL: ACW Press.

Thames, Earl (2014). *The Book of Revelation: A Commentary for Laypersons.* Bloomington, IN: Westbow Press.

Van Kampen, Robert (1992). *The Sign.* Wheaton, IL: Crossway Books.

Wallis, Jim (2015, Nov. 3). "Sojourners," *Huffington Post.*

Weaver, Richard (1948). *Ideas Have Consequences.* Chicago, IL: University of Chicago Press.

Williams, Paul L. (2007). *The Day of Islam: The Annihilation of America and the Western World.* Amherst, NY: Prometheus Books.

Chapter 4

Aisch, Gregor & Keller, Josh (2016, Mar. 18). "Gun Sales Soar," *NY Times.*

Ali, Abdullah Yusuf (2001). *The Meaning of the Holy Quran.* Beltsville, MD: Amana Corporation Publications.

Charles, J. Daryl (2005). *Between Pacifism and Jihad: Just War and Christian Tradition.* Westmont, IL: InterVarsity Press Academic.

Coughlin, Stephen (2015). *Catastrophic Failure: Blindfolding America in the Face of Jihad.* Seattle, WA: CreateSpace Independent Publishing Platform.

Dashti, 'Ali (1985). *Twenty three Years: A Study of the Prophetic Career of Mohammed*. Trans. from the Persian by F. R. C. Bagley. London: George Allen and Unwin.

Emerson, Steve (2002). *American Jihad: The Terrorists Living Among Us*. New York, NY: Free Press.

George, Robert P. (2001). *The Clash of Orthodoxies: Law, Religion, and Morality in Crisis*. Wilmington, DE: Intercollegiate Studies Institute.

Gerbner, G. & Gross, L. (1976). "Living with Television: The Violence Profile." *Journal of Communication*, 26, 76.

Gibb, H.A.R., Kramers, J.H (1953). *Shorter Encyclopaedia of Islam*. New York, NY: Cornell University Press.

Griswold, Eliza (2015, Jul. 22). "Is This the End of Christianity in the Middle East?" *New York Times Magazine*.

Hanson, Victor Davis (2015, Oct. 6). "The Iran Agreement Will Remake the Middle East — for the Worse." *National Review*.

Hartwig, Mark (2002a). *Citizen Magazine*, Vol. 16, No. 1, January.

Hartwig, Mark (2002b). "Spread by the Sword?" answeringislam.org.

Henry, Carl F. H. (1988). *Twilight of a Great Civilization: The Drift Toward Neo-Paganism*. Wheaton, IL: Crossway Books.

Houck, Chris (2015, Jul. 22). "ABC, NBC, and PBSS Censor Second Video Exposing Planned Parenthood Doc Selling." *Life News.*

Khan, Muhammed, M. (1997). *The Translation of the Meanings of Sahih Al-Bukhari: Arabic-English.* Chicago, IL: Kazi Publications.

Moore, Johnnie (2015). *Defying ISIS: Preserving Christianity in the Place of Its Birth and in Your Own Backyard.* Plano, TX: Thomas Nelson Publishers.

Moran, Rick (2015, Dec. 7). "ISIS Has Smuggled WMD Materials into Europe: EU Report." *American Thinker.*

Morey, Robert (1992). *The Islamic Invasion: Confronting the World's Fastest Growing Religion.* Eugene, OR: Harvest House Publishers.

Shafritz, Jay M. (1988). *The Dorsey Dictionary of American Government and Politics.* Belmont, CA: Dorsey Press.

Starkes, Teleeb (2013, Nov. 3). "Is a Race War Occurring?" *American Thinker.*

Williams, Paul L. (2007). *The Day of Islam: The Annihilation of America and the Western World.* Amherst, NY: Prometheus Books.

Chapter 5
Berman, D. (2015, Feb. 16). "Six Big Hack Attacks," *Think Advisor.*

Elias, Marilyn (2008, Jul. 23). "Economy's Stuck, But Business is Booming at Therapists' Offices." *USA Today*.

Goodman, Marc (2015). *Future Crimes: Everything Is Connected, Everyone Is Vulnerable and What We Can Do About It*. New York, NY: Knopf Doubleday Publishing Group.

Graham, Billy (1984). *Approaching Hoofbeats: The Four Horsemen of the Apocalypse*. New York, NY: Harper Collins.

Gwartney, James (2009). "The Economic Crisis of 2008. Cause and Aftermath." *James Madison Institute*.

Hayward, John (2015, May 20). "Cyberterrorism Is the Next 'Big Threat,' Says Former CIA Chief." *Breitbart*.

"Hunger & Poverty Factsheet." (2015). FeedingAmerica.org.

Huxley, Aldous (1932). *Brave New World*. London: Chatto & Windus.

Koppel, Ted (2015). *Lights Out: A Cyberattack, A Nation Unprepared, Surviving the Aftermath*. Danvers, MA: Crown Publishers.

Lifson, Thomas (2015, Jan. 29). "The Scariest Aspect of the Current Financial Crisis." *American Thinker*.

McManus, John. (1993). *Financial Terrorism: Hijacking America Under the Threat of Bankruptcy*. Jensen, UT: Jensen Book Publishers (Division of The John Birch Society).

Quigley, Carroll (1966). *Tragedy and Hope: A History of the World in Our Time*. London: Macmillan Publishers.

Rogers, Norm (2015, Jul. 20). "Let's Worry About a Real Threat." *American Thinker.*

"Slower Growth in Emerging Markets, a Gradual Pickup in Advanced Economies." (2015, Jul.) *International Monetary Fund Update.*

Snyder, Michael (2015, Oct. 20). "End of the American Dream." Endoftheamericandream.com.

Stewart, Tom (2008). "A Commentary on the Book of Revelation." whatsaiththescripture.com.

Troutman, Katey (2015, May 30). "From Farm to Table: 6 Reasons Why Food Costs So Damn Much." *Cheat Sheet.*

Worstall, Tim (2015, Feb. 20). "If We Knew Why WalMart Raised Wages Then We Could Decide Upon The Minimum Wage." *Forbes.*

Young, Angelo (2016, Jan. 7). "Dow Jones Industrial Plunges," *International Business Times.*

Zane, Kris (2014, Aug. 18). "Watch: Obama's Possible Plans To Use Military Force On The American People Just Got Exposed." *Western Journalism.*

"2015 World Hunger and Poverty Facts and Statistics." Worldhunger.org.

Chapter 6

"Ghost - Fourth Horseman Of The Apocalypse MSNBC - Egyptian Riots Original Full Video." (2011, Feb. 4). *Euronews*. Youtube.

Grant, S (2011). *In Defense of a Nation*. Bloomington, IN: Westbow Press.

Gregg, Steve (2013). *All You Want to Know About Hell: Three Christian Views of God's Final Solution to the Problem of Sin*. Plano, TX: Thomas Nelson Publishers.

Lalanilla, Marc (2014, Feb. 12). "Hungry for Humans: What's Behind Deadly Animal Attacks?" Livescience.com.

Chapter 7

Durkheim, Emile (1897). *Le Suicide*. Original Publisher: Unknown.

Donne, John (1609). "Holy Sonnet X: Death, Be Not Proud." Original Publisher: Unknown.

Foxe, John (1563). *Book of Martyrs: Actes and Monuments of these Latter and Perillous Days, Touching Matters of the Church*. New York, NY: John Day Publishing Company.

Johnston, Robert D. (1990). *Numbers in the Bible: God's Unique Design in Biblical Numbers*. Grand Rapids, MI: Kregel Publications.

Levinson, William (2014, May 31). May 31, 2013). "When You Have to Shoot, Shoot; Don't Talk." *American Thinker*.

Solzhenitsyn, Alexander (1978, Jun. 8). *A World Split Apart* — Commencement Address Delivered At Harvard University. Cambridge, MA.

Thomas, Dylan (1951). "Do Not Go Gentle into That Good Night." *Botteghe Oscure*.

Tzu, Sun (2017). *The Art of War Quotes*. San Francisco, CA: Goodreads, Inc.

Voshell, Fay (2015, May 10). "Persecution of Christians in America: It's Not Just 'Over There.'" *American Thinker*.

Chapter 8

Austin, Steve (2010). "Greatest Earthquakes of the Bible," *Acts & Facts*, 39 [10]: 12-15.

Biltz, Mark (2014). *Blood Moons: Decoding the Imminent Heavenly Signs*. WND Publishing. Washington, DC: WND Books.

Cahn, Jonathan (2014). *The Mystery of the Shemitah: The 3,000-Year-Old Mystery That Holds the Secret of America's Future*. Chicago, IL: Frontline Books.

Cisco, Taylor A., Jr. (2010). *All Shall Hide*. Bloomington, IN: Author House Self Publishing.

Goodman, Jeffrey (2010). *The Comets Of God-New Scientific Evidence for God: Recent Archeological, Geological and Astronomical Discoveries that Shine New Light on the Bible and its Prophecies*. Tuscon, AZ: Archeological Research Books, LLC.

Hitchcock, Mark (2014). *Blood Moons Rising: Bible Prophecy, Israel, and the Four Blood Moons*. Carol Stream, IL: Tyndale House Publishing.

Hohmann, Leo (2015, Apr. 3). "'Mystic' Rabbi Issues Ominous Warning on Eve of Blood Moon." *World Net Daily*.

Mack, Jay (2015). *Revelation, Where Life and the Bible Meet*. Nashville, TN: The Teaching Ministry of Jay Mack.

Chapter 9

Hill, Bob & McMahon (n.d.). "The Nature of The Mystery and The Rapture." *Theology Online*.

MacDonald, William (1995). *Believers Bible Commentary*. Nashville, TN: Thomas Nelson Publishers.

Rosenthal, Marvin (1990). *Prewrath Rapture of the Church*. Nashville, TN: Thomas Nelson Publishers.

Skurka, Jeffrey (2014, Oct. 10). "The Enigma of the Apparent Age of the Shroud of Turin." Theshroud.com.

Strong, James (2009). *Strong's Exhaustive Concordance of the Bible* (Online ed.). Peabody, MA: Hendrickson Publishers, Inc.

Chapter 10

Bork, Robert (1996). *Slouching Towards Gomorrah: Modern Liberalism and American Decline*. New York, NY: Harper Collins Publishers.

Filmer, W. E. (2011). *God Counts: A Study in Bible Numbers.* Mountain City, TN: Sacred Truth Publishing.

Yeats, William Butler (1920). *Michael Robartes and the Dancer.* Churchtown, Dundrum, Ireland: The Church Press.

Epilogue

Bennett, Dennis (1994). *The Holy Spirit and You: A Guide to the Spirit Filled Life.* Alachua, FL: Bridge-Logos Publishers.

Blamires, Harry (1963). *The Christian Mind. How Should a Christian Think?* London: Society for Promoting Christian Knowledge Publishers.

Ernst, Douglas (2016, Apr. 5). "ATM withdrawal limits stoke fears of financial meltdown." *World Net Daily.*

Gallups, Carl (2015). *Be Thou Prepared: Equipping the Church for Persecution and Times of Trouble.* Long Beach, CA: WND Books, Inc.

Hudson, F. Parker (1994). *On the Edge.* Atlanta, GA: Parker Hudson.

Kelly, Clifford W. (2016, Mar. 29). "On America at the Crossroads: Judgment or Mercy?" Facebook.

Kendrick, Alex (Director). (2015). *The War Room.* Albany, GA: Sherwood Pictures.

McCann, Steve (2016, Feb. 29). "The Closet Statist and the Constitutional Conservative." *American Thinker.*

Pascal, Blaise (c. 1650, 2013). *Pensées, part III, §233*. Seattle, WA: CreateSpace Independent Publishing Platform.

Peretti, Frank (1986). *This Present Darkness*. Wheaton, IL: Crossway Books.

Ramsey, Dave (2009). *The Total Money Makeover: A Proven Plan for Financial Fitness*. Nashville, TN: Thomas Nelson Publishers.

Russell, Neill G. (2015). *Newton's Riddle*. Mustang, OK: Tate Publishing and Enterprises, LLC.

Smith, C. Christopher (2014). "The Koinonia Way," *Christianity Today Leadership Journal*. August.

"The IMF Proposes 'Global Wealth Confiscation. The Appropriation of Household Savings.'" (2015, Apr. 3). *Global Research News*.

Thigpen, Paul (2014). *Manual for Spiritual Warfare*. Charlotte, NC: Tan Books, Lea Edition.

Tibbs, Scott (2009, Oct. 7). "Christians Are Called to Defend the Oppressed." ConservaTibbs.com/

About The Author

Dr. Cliff Kelly has served as Professor of Communication at several leading universities, both Christian and secular. During his long tenure as a teacher and scholar, he served briefly as Vice President of Strategic Initiatives for the International Fellowship of Christians and Jews. Dr. Kelly has also served as Senior Editor and Analyst for The Truth Project, Focus on the Family's worldwide Christian Worldview Outreach program. Formerly the founding Director of Academics for Focus on the Family Institute, Cliff served as administrator for all Institute faculty and academic programs and also taught the Christian Worldview Studies course, while serving as adjunct professor with Colorado Christian University. He received his bachelors and master's degrees from California State University at Long Beach, and his doctorate degree from Bowling Green State University (Ohio).

Dr. Kelly has also been a member of the faculty, most recently, at Liberty University, and also Regent University in Virginia, where he served as founding Director of the Institute of Public Affairs Journalism, teaching both journalism courses and political communication and leadership studies at the masters and doctoral student levels. He has lectured, written, and published in the areas of interpersonal and small group behavior, public policy, political journalism, intercultural and nonverbal communication, comparative worldview analysis, Biblical principles of human communication, organizational communication, and conflict resolution. While at Cleveland State, Professor Kelly received the Outstanding Young Teacher Award from the Central States Communication Association in 1975 and served as Assistant Dean of the College of Arts and Sciences.

Cliff has been married to Suzette Canete Kelly since 1981, and they have two grown children, Christina and Christopher. They now reside in Colorado Springs, Colorado. On a more personal level, Dr. Kelly accepted Jesus Christ as his Savior in 1979 in an Assemblies of God church in Stockton, California, at the age of 35. The family enjoys the company of two rescue pets,

Scout the Wonder Dog and Bianca the Black, plus the occasional visits from their daughter's dachshund, Pickle, and a newbie chihuahua named Jax "Petey Pablo" Chamaquito Rodriguez Kelly.

Dr. and Mrs. Kelly joyfully attend New Life Church in Colorado Springs.

Contact Dr. Kelly

EMAIL: kellysixthseal@gmail.com
PHONE: 719.481.1119

PUBLISHER

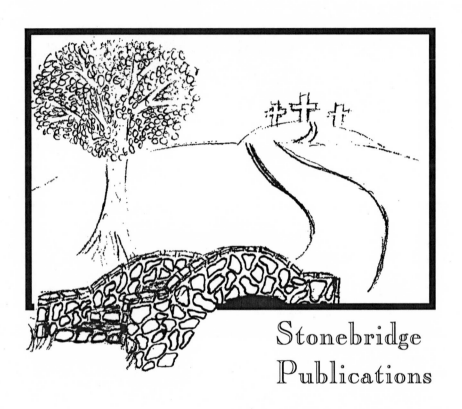

Stonebridge
Publications

FOR MORE GREAT TITLES, VISIT ONLINE AT:

STONEBRIDGEPUBLICATIONS.COM